BBC MUSIC GUIDES

SZYMANOWSKI

G000061514

BBC MUSIC GUIDES

Szymanowski

CHRISTOPHER PALMER

BRITISH BROADCASTING CORPORATION

Published by the
British Broadcasting Corporation
35 Marylebone High Street
London W1M 4AA

ISBN 0 563 20136 3

First published 1983

Filmset in Great Britain by
August Filmsetting, Warrington, Cheshire
Printed in England by Hollen Street Press, Slough, Berks

Contents

Preface

Karol Szymanowski was born in 1882 and died in 1937 at the age of fifty-five. In 1982 we celebrated the centenary of his birth; but had this event fallen due fifteen or even ten years ago we should have found precious little to celebrate it with. Hardly any records were available, scores and printed music were nearly all out of print, while the bibliography in English consisted solely of a few scattered articles by discriminating enthusiasts such as Felix Aprahamian and Kaikhosru Sorabji. Happily, much has now changed for the better. A fair cross-section of recordings is to be bought, both of British or American origin and those on the rather less accessible Polish *Muza* label; at the time of writing a good modern version of the *Stabat Mater* would be welcome, but the most notable omission from the catalogue is the song-cycles with orchestra, none of which have ever found their way on to disc. Universal Edition, Szymanowski's principal publishers, have reissued a large quantity of sheet music, and there are not one but *two* Collected Editions of his works under way under the general editorship of Teresa Chylińska: one in twenty-six volumes with introduction and notes only in Polish, the other in seventeen volumes with all editorial matter translated into German and English. (The prospective collector should be warned, however, that the two sets do not necessarily correspond in either the numbering of their volumes or the contents of the latter.) As for books and writings in English, Boguslaw Maciejewski followed up his pioneering biographical sketch of 1967 with a volume of Szymanowski's correspondence with the pianist Jan Smeterlin which included some of the composer's own writings on music. Teresa Chylińska's attractively produced pictorial biography appeared in 1964. Alistair Wightman's still unpublished doctoral thesis of 1972 has yielded a number of valuable articles in musical periodicals, and he is currently at work on a full-scale critical biography. The first comprehensive published study of the music was Jim Samson's, which came out as recently as 1980, lucidly written and wholly admirable in its blend of sympathy and critical discernment. Without Messrs. Wightman's and Samson's preliminary spadework my own task would have been immeasurably harder, and I gratefully acknowledge my debt to their efforts. My own work, however, is aimed at a less academically sophisticated readership than theirs, and while I have used music examples quite freely I have restricted abstruse technical talk to a minimum. I have not attempted to discuss every entry in Szymanowski's register of works (although most are at least mentioned somewhere), preferring instead to make generous allocations of space to what I regard as his major achievements.

I should like to express my gratitude to Alistair Wightman for permission to make use of information contained in his doctoral dissertation of 1972, for reading my text and making many invaluable comments and corrections; to Sylvia and Benjamin Shoshan for making some special translations from the Polish; to Stroma Sutherland, Robert Gilder and Dr H. Swiderska for patiently researching music, recordings and other material; and to Jill Burrows for her invaluable editorial and secretarial help.

C.P.
St John's Wood
May 1983

Biographical

Karol Maciej Szymanowski was born on 3 October 1882 on his family's estate at Tymoszówka in the Ukraine. He was the third of five children of a wealthy land-owning family who considered themselves Polish, although their lands had been under Russian jurisdiction since the partition of 1793. There was a history of musical accomplishment on both sides of the family, and all five children were artistic.

Karol's father, Stanislaw Korwin-Szymanowski, had inherited Tymoszówka from his father, along with some property in the neighbouring town of Elisavetgrad (now Kirovgrad). He embodied the tradition of the old Polish aristocracy: he was passionately patriotic, even though 'his' Poland had long ceased to exist on the map of Europe; he was cultured, well read and something of a dilettante in both the sciences and the arts. A talented pianist and cellist, he was impractical in everyday matters. Karol's mother, the Baroness Anna Taube, was of Swedish extraction, although her family had Polish connections for many generations. She, too, was a competent pianist and linguist, and outlived her son by six years.

The family estate at Tymoszówka might fit easily into a play by Chekhov or a novel by Turgenev. The large, rather sunless, house stood in the centre of the village, beside a lake, and was set in a spacious park. It was overshadowed by linden and walnut trees. A white porch, overgrown with vines, stretched the length of the one-storey building.

An accident to his left leg when he was four years old, and a subsequent series of operations on his left knee, left Karol with a pronounced limp and meant that he spent much of his childhood isolated at home, unable to attend school regularly. Books and music took the place of games, and he received most of his education from private tutors. Music was of vital importance within the household – even the dogs were given the names 'Scherzo' and 'Crotchet' – and Karol began to study the piano, under his father's direction, at the age of seven. After three years he was sent to his cousin Gustav Neuhaus's music school at Elisavetgrad where he could study piano and musical theory. Neuhaus soon realised his pupil's talent for composition and he introduced the boy not only to the music of Bach, Beethoven, Brahms and, naturally enough, Chopin, but also to Skryabin.

Both families, the Taubes on his mother's side and the Blumen-felds and Neuhauses on his father's, were thoroughly musical and prodigal of pianists, singers, composers and conductors. Karol's elder brother Feliks became a pianist and composer of light music; his younger sister Stanislawa (Stasia) had considerable success as a soprano and frequently performed her brother's music. (She, too, outlived him, but only by a year.) The atmosphere of Tymoszówka was bright and social. There were frequent dances and parties at which music would be made and plays and pantomimes performed. The two neighbouring estates were also rich in musical associations, since Leo Davidov of Verbovka was Tchaikovsky's brother-in-law and Dmitri Davidov of Kamienka his nephew. (Dmitri's brother was Vladimir, Tchaikovsky's beloved 'Bob', the dedicatee of the *Pathétique*, who had committed suicide in 1906.) By contrast Elisavetgrad could offer the young composer very little in the way of musical stimulus. However, a touring opera company did visit the town twice a year, and we know that Szymanowski saw Glinka's *Ruslan and Ludmila*, Dargomizhsky's *Rusalka* and Weber's *Oberon*. He saw *Carmen* and *Lohengrin* in Vienna and brought back home all the available piano scores of Wagner's operas.

Szymanowski had been composing, mainly for the piano, from the age of about ten, and his first published work was a set of nine Chopinesque miniatures, the *Preludes*, Op. 1, written during his late teens. In 1901 his father decided to send him to Warsaw for further study, and he took private lessons from Zawirski and Noskowski.

Even by the standards of the time, Warsaw was insular and backward-looking. The growth of music education had been slow, and although there were opera-houses and theatres, few professional orchestras or chamber music groups existed. The critics were conservative in outlook and the audiences apathetic. Musically the clock had stopped with Chopin and Moniuszko (1819–1872), whose music embodied a nostalgic patriotism that was as much political as aesthetic in origin. For over a century Poland had been a pawn on the European chessboard. It had been partitioned three times within a quarter of a century, for the last time in 1793 when Russia had taken control of that part of the Ukraine in which the Szymanowskis' estates lay, Austria the south-west region and Prussia the north-west. Here was a recipe for discontent and a desperate, impassioned nationalism that showed itself violently both in militant action (in, for example, the uprising of 1863) and, no less markedly, in the arts.

Despite a crushing censorship literature acknowledged an obligation to indigenous Polish history and culture, and music leaned towards the use of national idioms such as the polonaise and the mazurka. The price of nationalism in the creative arts was a freezing of natural growth and development and an ignorance – almost a denial – of the progressive currents gaining momentum elsewhere in Europe. Wagner and Strauss flourished in Germany and Debussy in France; but Warsaw remained firmly within the classical tradition of Mendelssohn and Chopin.

In Warsaw Szymanowski not only received a reasonably thorough grounding in compositional techniques from Noskowski (a former pupil of Moniuszko), but also made contact with the small group of friends who were to remain closely associated all their lives: Artur Rubinstein the pianist, Paweł Kochański the violinist, and Grzegorz Fitelberg the composer and conductor. Rubinstein gave many first performances of Szymanowski's piano works. Fitelberg ('Ficiu') abandoned composition in favour of conducting and gave countless Szymanowski premières throughout the composer's life. He was essentially practical and had the invaluable talent of knowing the right people at the right time. It was, for instance, through Fitelberg that Szymanowski signed with the Viennese publishers, Universal Edition. (This association foundered in the 1930s and major late works such as *Harnasie* and the *Symphonie Concertante* were published by Max Eschig of Paris.) It was also through Fitelberg that Szymanowski came to know Kochański, who had been a child prodigy and was now a member of the Warsaw Philharmonic. Kochański's playing inspired two of Szymanowski's masterpieces, *Mythes* and the First Violin Concerto.

Szymanowski and Fitelberg joined with two more of Noskowski's composition students, Ludomir Różycki and Apolinary Szeluto, to form the group known as 'Młoda Polska' ('Young Poland in Music'). The group was loosely modelled on the parallel 'Young Poland in Literature' movement which consisted of like-minded, energetic young creative artists with a progressive outlook and semi-bohemian life-style. Szymanowski continued to write for the piano, and also began to set a number of poems by contemporary Polish writers such as Kazimierz Tetmajer, Jan Kasprowicz, Waclaw Berent and Tadeusz Miciński. Różycki describes Szymanowski at this time composing at the keyboard (something he continued to do throughout his life) and, while working on his First Piano Sonata, studying in great detail the music of Chopin and Skryabin. His father, who died in 1906, was his careful and tireless copyist.

Młoda Polska acquired, in the person of Prince Władysław Lubomirski, then a pupil of Fitelberg, a welcome and generous patron. With his help the young musicians were able to set up The Polish Composers' Press and to promote concerts of their own music, performed by members of the group, in the major cities of Poland and Germany. Initially Młoda Polska met with great success in Warsaw, its first major concert being given on 2 February 1906 and including works by Szymanowski, Różycki, Fitelberg, Karłowicz and Szeluto. Performances of Szymanowski's *Concert Overture*, and of his Variations, Op. 10, and B flat minor Etude, Op. 4 no. 3 (played by his cousin Henryk Neuhaus), drew from Warsaw's leading critic of the day, Aleksander Poliński, such rapturous phrases as 'talent of no common order' and 'stamp of genius'. Sadly, little more than a year later Poliński changed his tune, his own 'nationalism' closing his ears and making him antagonistic to the now German-influenced music of Młoda Polska.

The years between the establishment of Młoda Polska and the outbreak of the First World War were a time of travel and musical exploration. Szymanowski spent much of this period commuting between Tymoszówka, Warsaw and Vienna, where he kept a flat for some years. He seemed for ever undecided about whether he wanted to be isolated in the countryside or surrounded by friends in the city, whether he wanted to apply himself to composition and ignore everything apart from his music, or to criss-cross Europe as if on some everlasting aristocratic grand tour, travelling first class and staying in the best hotels, while he had scarcely a penny to his name and was constantly juggling his debts, borrowing from Peter to pay Paul.

It was in an attempt to raise funds that in 1908 he started work on an operetta, *Lottery for a Husband*, to a libretto by Julian KrzewińskiMaszyński. As light music and as a money-spinner it was doomed to failure, and was never published or performed in the composer's lifetime. More congenial was the writing of song-cycles to words by various German poets. Then in March 1909 his two-movement First Symphony received its first and last performance. It was received coldly and Szymanowski withdrew it, describing it as a 'contrapuntal-harmonic-orchestral monster'. A trio for violin, cello and piano suffered a similar fate. More successful were the Second

Symphony (first performed by Fitelberg in Warsaw in April 1911) and the Second Piano Sonata, started in 1910 and given by Rubinstein in Berlin in December 1911. Both works were well received also elsewhere in Europe.

The hold that German culture had on Szymanowski began to weaken in 1910 and 1911 with two trips to Italy and Sicily in the company of his great friend Stefan Spiess. In December 1910 he wrote to his friend and biographer, Zdzisław Jachimecki:

If Italy did not exist I could not exist either. I am not a painter or a sculptor, but when I contemplate these proud, imperious works gazing down serenely and with an indulgent smile at everything that is base, stupid and soulless – when I think about these generations of the greatest, the most marvellous geniuses, I feel that life and work are worth something.

Despite a growing disenchantment with Strauss he returned in his opera *Hagith* of 1912 to *Salome* and *Elektra* for inspiration. But by 1913 his disillusion with German romanticism was complete. Szymanowski had made a new discovery: 'Stravinsky is a genius!' he wrote to Spiess. 'I am terribly impressed with his work and *par conséquence* am becoming indifferent to German music.' During a visit by Rubinstein to Tymoszówka later in the year, the two played together the two-piano arrangement of *Petrushka* which Szymanowski had seen danced by Diaghilev's Ballets Russes in Vienna.

In January 1914 Szymanowski visited Zakopane in the Tatra Mountains with Rubinstein. The region was of particular importance to young Polish musicians and writers, including the poet Miciński and the playwright Witkiewicz, and an artistic colony had been established there. Szymanowski found the atmosphere excessively intellectual and, although the indigenous music of the Tatra Mountains was to assume an importance for his music in later years, his interests were more readily aroused by the South and the East.

Because of his worsening financial plight, which obliged him to give up the Vienna flat, Szymanowski was unable to make another visit to Italy in the spring of 1913; but in 1914 he undertook a major foreign tour, taking in Italy and Sicily once more as well as Algiers, Constantine, Biskra and Tunis. The trip renewed and intensified his interest in exotic cultures and he began to compile notebooks on the history and culture of the Arab world. He wrote from Biskra on 11 April 1914, 'This place is divine.'

Later, in May 1914, Szymanowski set out for Paris and London. In both cities he appears to have been lionised by society hostesses like Muriel Draper who specialised in peopling their salons with visiting composers. In Paris he spent much time with Rubinstein and the thriving community of Polish artists surrounding Cyprian Godebski who brought Szymanowski into contact with many of the leading representatives of contemporary French culture. Frequent guests at the Godebskis' included Ravel, Debussy, Cocteau and Gide, as well as Stravinsky himself.

On 14 June 1914 Archduke Ferdinand was assassinated at Sarajevo. War was inevitable. Szymanowski declined Paderewski's invitation to Switzerland and cut short his planned visit to Vienna. Europe was in a turmoil of uncertainty, and he reached Tymoszówka by the very last normal peacetime train service.

Szymanowski's poor health exempted him from conscription into the Tsarist army, and until the Bolshevik Revolution broke out he spent the war years quietly at Tymoszówka. This was the most fruitful creative period of his life. He had a rough little hut – his 'Kompozytornia' – built a little way from the house, and would spend up to ten hours a day there composing, as he had always done, at the piano. During this period were written the First Violin Concerto, the Third Symphony, *Masques, Métopes* and *Mythes*. The pull of the Near East was still strong, even though all opportunities for travel were now curtailed. While engaged on the Third Symphony, Szymanowski wrote nostalgically to Spiess: 'I lately had a mania for constantly recalling where we had been at this time last year. When I got hold of my African and Sicilian pictures in Tymoszówka, I was quite overcome with emotion. . . .'

Early in 1915 he was offered, by Glière, the post of Professor of Composition at Kiev Conservatory. It carried a salary of 2000 roubles a month, a considerable attraction for the now-impecunious composer, and it took Szymanowski some little time to resist the temptation and decline the offer. He could not at this time bring himself to sacrifice his freedom; when later events forced him to do so the results were disastrous.

Troubles began in earnest when the aristocratic, albeit straitened, lifestyle of the Tymoszówka estate was swept away for ever with the 1917 Revolution. At first Szymanowski believed it would be possible to continue much as before. However Tymoszówka was destroyed and with it much invaluable Szymanowski autograph material and correspondence. (Yet more documentation was destroyed in

Warsaw during the Second World War.) The family was soon obliged to settle in Elisavetgrad, a town Szymanowski disliked intensely. He was never again able to own even a piano of his own, and for the rest of his life had to compose on hired instruments.

Although he continued to compose, putting the finishing touches to the Third Piano Sonata and his First String Quartet, Szymanowski now turned his attention to his homosexual novel *Ephebos*, which took him two years to write. He had not wished it to be published during his mother's lifetime, and it is believed that the manuscript, which was entrusted to Jarosław Iwaszkiewicz, perished during the 1939–45 war. (Recently some 150 pages have turned up in Paris in a Russian translation, and this may by no means be the end of the story.) The opera *King Roger* was also begun during the war years (in 1918) but not completed until 1924. The sample from *Ephebos* given in English translation on page 33 clearly demonstrates the closeness of stylistic relationship that exists between novel and opera; both have strong personal connotations.

In 1919, after the Szymanowski family had had several near escapes from rioting peasants, the Red Army finally entered the Ukraine. In March Kiev was occupied by German forces and Odessa and Elisavetgrad were seized by the Austrians. The family eventually managed to sell their Elisavetgrad property for a fraction of its value, and on Christmas Eve 1919 Szymanowski arrived in Warsaw, now the capital of free, independent Poland. For his first year there Szymanowski was a guest of the Spiess family. Chamber concerts were arranged in Warsaw, Cracow and Lwow, with Kochański playing *Mythes* and the Op. 9 Sonata, and Szymanowski accompanying Stasia in the *Songs of an Infatuated Muezzin* and some of the Hafiz songs. The concerts in Lwow and Cracow were reasonably well attended, but the Warsaw reception was a major disappointment for Szymanowski. He wrote to Jachimecki on 31 January 1920: 'In Warsaw there were not even 600 people interested in knowing what I have done during the past six years! . . . I am a stranger to them, incomprehensible . . . and a good-for-nothing. . . . To hell with them all.'

The years between 1918 and 1922 were years of transition for Szymanowski. He was now rediscovering his own musical roots, absorbing indigenous Polish culture, particularly its folk music; from his personal brand of ecstatic orientalism he moved to a natural awareness of his Polish identity and the folk-culture of his own people. The changeover was decisive by 1923 with the publication of *Słopiewnie*, a cycle of five songs to poems by the Polish poet Julian Tuwim. All this time he was persevering with *King Roger*, a work that belongs essentially to an earlier phase in his creative life. Already in 1920 he was writing that he was 'sick and tired of my "Shepherd"'. In retrospect, Szymanowski himself saw these few years as crucial in his development. He wrote in 1927 to Jachimecki:

I am concerned with one evolutionary point with which I would like to acquaint you, namely the lechitic[1], ancestral Polish character, which you discerned in the *Słopiewnie*. It was indeed a turning-point, starting a development continuing through the *Mazurkas* . . . the *Stabat Mater* and a new ballet [*Harnasie*] on which I am now working. I believe this to be a point which should be stressed and analysed in depth. I am concerned, myself, with crystallising elements of tribal heritage.

Meanwhile he completed a commission for a one-act *Commedia dell'Arte*-style ballet, *Mandragora*, which received its first performance in 1920, and later that year he and Jan Effenberg-Sliwiński were sent by the Polish Government on a 'cultural mission' to Paris, Copenhagen, Oslo, Stockholm and London in order to encourage and promote concerts and exhibitions of Polish art. Szymanowski however opted out of the Scandinavian part. Leaving Effenberg-Sliwiński in Paris, he spent November in London with the Kochańskis and renewed his friendship with Artur Rubinstein. Violinist, pianist and composer set sail from Liverpool on 15 January 1921 for New York. Rubinstein, a natural promoter and publicist, found Szymanowski's reticence a challenge:

Karol was not easy to handle. He suffered from agoraphobia and was exceedingly reserved with strangers. He also had an aversion to showing his works to musicians who had not already heard of him. He would say, 'I hate to pass exams at my age!' All this did not make my task easy, but he had the confidence of a child in both of us; he felt safe in our company.

Szymanowski's own reaction to New York was predictable. He wrote to his family on 2 February 1921: 'We have been here a week and, of course, there is a mass of impressions. . . . [We] are already aware . . . that this may be a good place to visit, for dollars – but to live here, God forbid!' In March, Szymanowski and Rubinstein travelled to Boston, Philadelphia, Florida and Cuba, which latter, in particular, greatly excited the composer: 'It's altogether a fabulous

---

[1] Lech was the legendary founder, the 'protoplast', of the Polish race.

place! . . . the typical charm of the South and of the Latin race! I am in heaven!'

After a second trip to New York in September 1921, Szymanowski returned to Europe in March 1922. The opera *Hagith* had its long-delayed première at Warsaw Opera House in May of that year, but was dropped after only a handful of performances. Szymanowski spent the winter of 1922–3 in Zakopane which he now somewhat belatedly 'discovered'. Zakopane had become famous in the mid-nineteenth century as a health resort, developing with the arrival of the railway line into a tourist centre and the spiritual home for a community of artists and writers fascinated by the folk culture of the Tatra Mountains. Szymanowski entered fully into its spirit and appears to have been warmly welcomed by the mountain people. Rubinstein has left an enticing picture of Zakopane in *My Young Years*:

The countryside was enchanting, with the river Dunajec roaring down from the heights, its pure and transparent water jumping over rocks and stones . . . dark, tall pine forests surrounded the village . . . the shapes of the mountains suggested fairy tales; mysterious and aloof, they looked forbidding to outsiders, but not to their own native sons, the Tatra mountaineers, a singular, original race who, quite unlike other Poles, lived in close contact with the mountains. Lean and tall, their faces like eagles, with high cheekbones and curved noses, mostly clean-shaven, they looked like ideal models for painters and sculptors.

And for composers too: Szymanowski celebrates them in his ballet-pantomime *Harnasie*.

For the next fifteen years Szymanowski divided his time between the Tatra Mountains and Warsaw. Four major works were written during this period: the *Stabat Mater*, *Harnasie*, the Second Violin Concerto and the Fourth Symphony for piano and orchestra (*Symphonie Concertante*). He made occasional trips to Paris where his work was beginning to be quite frequently performed and warmly received. His First String Quartet received its first performance in Warsaw in April 1924 and in June 1926 *King Roger*, completed in 1924, was staged in Warsaw with Stasia Szymanowska as Roxana. Szymanowski found Warsaw, and the flat he was sharing with August Iwanski, increasingly noisy and uncongenial and during the late 1920s spent as much time as he could in Zakopane.

Late in 1926, Szymanowski was offered simultaneously two important education posts: Principal of the Warsaw Conservatory and Director of the Cairo Conservatory. The salary offered by the

Egyptians was much larger and the climate there would have been better for his health – he was as yet unaware that he was suffering from advanced tuberculosis as well as possibly cancer of the lungs and throat. He finally accepted the Warsaw post, saying, 'I prefer to be a pauper in Poland than a rich man elsewhere!'

He had developed strong ideas on the theory of education and the direction he wanted the Conservatory to take in the future. He arrived there like the proverbial new broom, making sweeping changes and bitter enemies in a matter of days. In April 1927 he wrote to Zofia Kochańska:

> . . . already in the first month I managed to make changes in the charter allowing me complete freedom of action. I can now do exactly as I like without consulting the Board. . . . I face the tremendous task of completely reorganising the Conservatory. There is, of course, a group that welcomes me. . . . The rest . . . are very polite, but hate me at heart. . . . There will be terrible conflicts before the end of term, because I intend simply to fire several of them, *ohne Weiteres*. . . .

Both the strain of trying to drag the Conservatory overnight into the twentieth century and his gradually worsening state of health began to take their toll. Szymanowski regularly smoked sixty a day, and particularly during his frequent bouts of depression could drink considerable quantities of vodka. There is also evidence to suggest that he might have been a morphine or cocaine addict as well as, to all intents and purposes, an alcoholic. He was sent to the sanatorium at Edlach in mid-December 1928 and stayed there until the end of February 1929. In July he resigned from the Conservatory and in mid-September moved from Edlach to Davos where he remained until the following May. In September 1930 he moved into a four-roomed log cottage in Zakopane, known as 'Atma', with a male servant and a housekeeper. Slowly his health began to improve and he was able to take up the post of Rector of the newly established State Academy of Music in Warsaw. His tenure was to be short: a new Minister of Education dismissed him in 1932 and disbanded the Academy completely a year later.

In 1930 Szymanowski received the Polish State Prize for Music and, at the end of the same year, an honorary PhD from the University of Cracow. At long last he was able to feel, if only briefly, that he was gaining some recognition in his own country; suddenly he felt a need to complete all his unfinished works, including *Harnasie*, the *Symphonie Concertante*.

Despite his recent honours, Szymanowski was still depressed by his lack of standing in his homeland. However, as part of the 1932 Annual Polish Choral Festival at Poznań it was planned to mark his fiftieth birthday with performances of the *Stabat Mater* and the *Symphonie Concertante*. He was invited to give a speech at the dinner in his honour, but had to decline on grounds of ill-health since by this time he could barely whisper. Once again his financial difficulties had reached crisis point, and the ailing composer was obliged to travel abroad, giving one concert tour after another in order to support himself and his family. In 1933 alone he visited Warsaw, Copenhagen, Madrid, Paris, Bologna, Russia, Yugoslavia, Bulgaria and Hungary. Despairingly, he wrote to Iwaszkiewicz: 'Lately my life is full of sorrow, misfortune, illness and work. I have to play a lot (the piano) which I do not like, as you well know.' In September 1934, he wrote to Stasia, 'I have absolutely nothing. Every day I borrow a few zloty from friends.' The award of the Commander's Cross of Polonia Restituta from the Polish Government did little to revive his flagging spirits.

Jan Smeterlin was arranging a series of concerts for him in England. Szymanowski, at his lowest ebb, wrote to his promoter on 14 September 1934, begging him to arrange some extra musical 'at homes' during the London visit. He was destitute and in despair. He describes himself as 'a down-and-out whore . . . capable of selling myself for any price'. Can Smeterlin find a buyer for the manuscript of the *Symphonie Concertante*? The tuberculosis has recurred, but he cannot afford to take the cure, as he is the sole financial support for his mother and two of his sisters and their children. His bitterness towards the Polish authorities is as strong as ever. He is so depressed that he even hints at the possibility of suicide: 'These requests will apply only if I am still alive in October. Unfortunately this sentence sounds a little melodramatic, but this time I am serious. . . . I have reached a stage where one no longer reasons sanely; decisions are easily made. . . . One tires and one loses the urge to live.'

The English tour went ahead and included a BBC broadcast of the *Symphonie Concertante* conducted by Malcolm Sargent. Writing in 1967, Felix Aprahamian remembered turning pages for the composer at a musical evening at the home of Mrs Gertrude Hopkins – evidently Smeterlin had succeeded in arranging a few 'at homes':

I remember him as a sensitive, nervous and not invariably accurate pianist. . . . [He] struck me as a very harassed man. I wondered at the time what the composer of *La Fontaine d'Aréthuse* could possibly have to worry about. Reading the heart-rending letter he wrote to Jan Smeterlin has now, after more than thirty years, helped me to understand that he had more to distress him than a few wrong notes . . . his posthumous glory in the land of his birth can never erase the terrible indictment of that letter.

In December 1934, as part of a 'cultural exchange' arranged by the Polish and German Governments, Szymanowski was sent to Berlin for a series of concerts to be conducted by Wilhelm Furtwängler. He arrived only to find that Furtwängler had been ordered by the Nazi authorities to make a substitution for a piece by the 'decadent' Hindemith. Furtwängler refused and resigned. Szymanowski declined to play under a replacement conductor and returned home. In March 1935 he took the *Symphonie Concertante* to Stockholm, Oslo, Bergen and Copenhagen, and in May to Riga where he was made Honorary Professor at the Conservatory. He travelled on from Riga to Prague for the (very successful) première of *Harnasie*. A series of rows, suspensions and mishaps delayed the Paris performances (with Serge Lifar as Harnas and choreography by Jan Cieplinski, who had been responsible for that of Bartók's *Miraculous Mandarin* and *Duke Bluebeard's Castle* at the Budapest Opera) from November 1935 to April 1936, but the composer was pleased with it when it did take place. He spent January and February 1936 in the Helios sanatorium at Grasse and March at the Palace Grand Hotel. Towards the end of the year he was able to return there, although he could afford only a modest hotel and not the sanatorium which he really needed. He hired a piano, but composed little; he read, listened to the radio and enjoyed the sounds of the children playing nearby.

He was last seen in public at a concert in Cannes given by Artur Rubinstein. Three laryngologists examined him and gave him only six months to live. He was transferred temporarily to a clinic in Lausanne, the intention being to move him on to the sanatorium at Lugano after Easter. However, the doctor at Lausanne realised that Szymanowski would not survive the journey and sent immediately for Stasia. He died just before midnight on 29 March 1937 with Stasia and his secretary, Leonia Gradstein, at his bedside.

When Artur Rubinstein heard of his friend's death he raised enough money to arrange a decent funeral, but found that matters were being taken care of, ironically but just as Szymanowski had predicted, by the Polish Government:

. . . the authorities trumpeted pompously the tragic loss of their great son.

They prepared a Warsaw funeral with an unheard-of mass of publicity. A hundred thousand people were tightly massed to watch the funeral. A special train transported his body, accompanied by ministers and the family, to Cracow for the grand burial at the church at Skalka, where only the greatest of the nation were allowed to lie. They put on the catafalque the insignia of the Grand Cross of Polonia Restituta, the nation's highest honour. What a bitter irony! For years they had made my poor Karol suffer through their meanness and now they were willing to spend a fortune on this big show. And what really infuriated me was the fact that they asked Hitler's government to make the train with Karol's body stop in Berlin long enough to receive military honours.[1]

Perspective

Szymanowski's creative life is generally (and conveniently) divided into three main periods: (i) 1899–1913, when he was 'working through' the influences of Chopin, Skryabin and the late German romantics; (ii) 1914–18, which admitted the Impressionists and Stravinsky and produced most of the works by which Szymanowski is likely to be remembered; and (iii) about 1921–33, characterised by a new 'nationalist' awareness which manifested itself chiefly in a use of folk music and other traditional sources. These are the broad outlines; much within them calls for explanatory comment. A certain amount of juvenilia predates 1899 and is lost; thereafter, however, a disconcertingly large number of works are listed as either unfinished, unpublished or lost, among them the First Symphony (1906–7), the operetta *Lottery for a Husband* (1908–9), the cantata *Agave* (1917), the ballet *Mandragora* (1920), the Piano Concerto (1924–5), the Piano Concertino (1934) – not to mention the novels *Ephebos* (1918–19), *Tom, or the Adventures of a Polish Boy on Land and Sea* (1921) and *The Tale of the Itinerant Juggler and the Seven Stars* (1921). This represents a sizeable body of work when we remember that Szymanowski was by no means a facile or prolific composer. His natural fastidiousness led him never to persist in mining a vein once it was exhausted, and to shun excessive lengths. Years went by during which he hardly composed anything of substance – the last three years of his life, for instance, when he was too sick and harassed by money worries to write. Needless to say, the boundaries between compartments are

[1] *My Many Years.*

not watertight: *King Roger* (1918–24) bestrides the end of the second period and the beginning of the third, and transitional works like the *Love Songs of Hafiz* (1911) and the First String Quartet (1917) amalgamate a variety of elements. Similarly, Szymanowski in the midst of one period occasionally reverts to formal and linguistic idioms associated with another. The Twelve Studies, Op. 33 (1916), and the Third Piano Sonata (1917) both date from the 'Impressionistic' second period but look back to the 'classicism' of the first; and two late works, the Joyce Songs of Op. 54 (1926) and the first of the *Two Mazurkas*, Op. 62 (1933–4), both refer the listener to the 'Impressionist' period when the composer's interest in harmony and timbre *per se* was livelier than it subsequently became. What the pigeon-hole method of classification always tends to obscure is the view of the picture as a whole, the logical, inevitable process of evolutionary growth and development which it is particularly important to recognise in the case of a composer like Szymanowski whose eclecticism might otherwise create a misleading impression.

It was fitting that, for a composer whose long-term ambition was to bring Polish music into a European context as a competitive entity, his published, 'official' Opus 1 should be the nine *Preludes*

Ex.1 Prelude, Op.1, no.4

for piano (1899–1900) though two of them, nos. 7 and 8, were composed when he was only fourteen. Ex. 1 shows a typical extract, the overmastering influence being Chopin, who laid the foundation for a Polish nationalist tradition which his immediate successors failed to build upon, or were prevented by political circumstances from so doing. Like Chopin, Szymanowski was an aristocrat, in art as in life, not merely by accident of birth but in the wider, truer sense. Chopin made beauty of sound and textural clarity his special concern, for his responses were primarily simple, sensuous and passionate; it was this, together with his almost exclusive preoccupation with personal sensation, that led him to the discovery of novel ways of thinking and feeling musically, both harmonically and in the sphere of form. Chopin too was a Slav, with the almost fanatical devotion to the land of their birth characteristic of the Slavonic peoples, and Polish peasant elements are continually bursting into the rarefied atmosphere of the Parisian *salon*. These are all features destined to reappear at a somewhat later stage of evolution in Szymanowski's music and entitle us to regard him as one of Chopin's legitimate heirs.

Chopin and also Chopin-through-Skryabin is easily enough identified in the *Four Studies*, Op. 4 (1900–2). No. 3, in B flat minor, was made famous by Paderewski and has remained one of the composer's most popular pieces. The salon-derived feeling of claustrophobic preciousness in those preludes and studies is no more palatable in Szymanowski than in Skryabin or in Chopin himself, but in Szymanowski's case it was quickly outgrown. Skryabin, however, though touched on lightly in Op. 4 and the object of much close attention on Szymanowski's part at this time, comes to play a much more significant role in the latter's music during the coming 'Impressionist' period. The Variations, Op. 3 (1901–3), are more dependent on classical models, but Op. 10 – the *Variations on a Polish Theme* (1900–4) – recalls Chopin's pre-Impressionism, particularly in the eighth variation, a 'Marcia funebre' underpinned throughout by a deep dissonant booming of bells; and in the finale, whose coda shimmers with trills and tremolos in such a manner as to anticipate the florid textures and polychrome piano 'orchestration' of the middle-period *Mythes*, *Métopes* and *Masques*.

Seeds of contact with aboriginal Polish folk music are sown in the Op. 5 songs to poems by Jan Kasprowicz (1902); but broadly speaking the language of these early settings of the 'Young Poland' poets – i.e. of Tetmajer (Op. 2) and Miciński (Op. 11 and Op. 20) – is Germanic rather than Polish. Try as he might – and in later years he went so far as to denounce it publicly in articles – Szymanowski never succeeded totally in extricating himself from the complex chromatic toils of late-German romanticism, i.e. the language of Wagner, Wolf, Strauss, Reger, Mahler. So it was only to be expected that in the songs of Op. 13 (1905–7), Op. 17 (1907) and Op. 22 (1910), he should be setting German rather than Polish texts, and that his early orchestral style should be heavily indebted to Strauss. The *Concert Overture* after a poem by Miciński (1904–5) is altogether too derivative to be called a good piece (although it need not sound quite as crude as it does were conductors not too lazy or too unmusical to modify the heavy brass dynamics in accordance with present-day orchestral requirements[1]) and Alistair Wightman, who has examined the manuscript of the incomplete and unpublished First Symphony, describes its orchestration as 'heavily scored, even by the standards of *c*. 1910–20'. The one-act opera *Hagith* (1912–13) leans primarily on *Salome* and *Elektra*, influences later to reappear in thoroughly assimilated form in Szymanowski's operatic masterpiece, *King Roger*. These works are mentioned here but not selected for detailed discussion later, since none of them represents the mature Szymanowski. (Exception is made in the case of the Second Symphony (1909–10), which sums up in acceptable enough form most of the characteristics of this early period, and of the *Love Songs of Hafiz*, an important transitional work.) German classicism gave Szymanowski a command of form and of counterpoint which was to stand him in excellent stead throughout his life; romanticism provided him with a basic vocabulary of expression. The next stage was to enlarge and refine upon those acquisitions and to admit a new (though related)

---

[1] It is almost certain that contemporary brass instruments make considerably more sound than their turn-of-the-century counterparts; hence the need for constant vigilance in the performance of unedited scores.

world of influence: the resulting blend would be more than the sum of its constituent parts and would, in fact, constitute the mature, the real, Szymanowski.

The young composer's interest in German musical culture began to decline steeply as a result of his travels with Stefan Spiess, first to Southern Italy and Sicily in April 1911, then to Sicily and North Africa in 1914. Betwixt times he composed the first of his orientally inspired song-cycles, the *Love Songs of Hafiz*, the first clear indication of his oncoming mature style. It is possible that, like Gide before him, these journeys into exotic lands where forbidden fruit was freely to be had (especially by well-to-do foreigners) enabled him to realise the true direction of his sexual impulses, and that this affected in no small way the blossoming of his creative personality. Szymanowski made no overt declaration of his homosexuality in his music; *King Roger* is the only work in which any kind of homoerotic element is to be discerned, and his treatment of it is unsensational and unself-conscious. Rather is it his two-volume novel *Ephebos* which is described by Maciejewski as Szymanowski's 'apologia pro vita sua'. As we shall see, one of the predominant influences on both Szymanowski's thought and, so far as can be determined, his literary style was Walter Pater, whose unacknowledged homosexuality undoubtedly favoured his interest in ancient Greece. Some account needs to be taken of this matter, for a form of sexual liberation is surely implicit in the pronouncedly 'Dionysian' impulse which activates so many works of the middle period. Dionysus was the god of wine, fertility and the art of music, and largely through Nietzsche – a writer Szymanowski adored, considering *The Birth of Tragedy* 'one of the most beautiful books in the world' – Szymanowski became an ardent disciple. The orgies of Dionysus, with his attendant satyrs and leopards, are described in the *Bacchae* (one of the sources of *King Roger*'s libretto); Dionysus inflames that spirit of drunken ecstasy, of intoxicated spiritual and bodily abandon, in which, according to Nietzsche, man most perfectly realises his own highest nature. In this 'pagan' ecstasy man says 'Yes' to life as it is, without trying to separate good from evil. Zarathustra's Dionysian 'yea-saying' is the 'joyful wisdom' (*Die Fröhliche Wissenschaft*) which cannot be expressed in arguments, only in the ecstasy of song and dance. Now Dionysus (or Pan) is a recurrent figure in Szymanowski's work of this period – in 'Dryades et Pan' (No. 3 of *Mythes*), in the Miciński poem on which the First Violin Concerto is based ('Pan plays on his pipes in the oak-grove'); finally and most critically in *King Roger*, where he becomes incarnate as one of the two principal *dramatis personae*. Even more pervasive are the twin manifestations of the Dionysian impulse, the song and the dance.

Although so-called 'civilised' man thinks of speaking as natural and singing as artificial, song to primitive, uncorrupted man was a natural and spontaneous expression of emotion, of the urge to transcend himself. Speech began with song just as literature began with poetry. Song is the natural, the arch-natural expression of man's ecstasy or rapture, that is to say his 'Dionysian' joy in the world, in the creation and contemplation of beauty. Song, therefore, is the heart and soul of all music, and Szymanowski reaffirms its supremacy. Even in the relatively few works of this period in which voices themselves are not involved 'song' is still to the fore: through the medium of the violin (bardic in *Mythes*, skylark- or nightingale-like in the First Violin Concerto) or of the piano as it evokes the song of the Sirens in *Métopes*, the song of Sheherazade in *Masques*.

As for the dance, it too from time immemorial has been a symbol of ecstasy. It causes man to lose his individual consciousness and merge in oneness with the Universe, with the Godhead. In ancient Greece dancing was part of every child's education. Lucian, a Greek Christian writer of the second century, claimed that Orpheus had prescribed dancing to anyone who was to be introduced to the wisdom of the 'mysteries'. Alistair Wightman suggests that Szymanowski's preoccupation with the dance could be a form of psychological compensation for his physical disability (in childhood he had contracted undiagnosed tuberculosis of the bones which caused him to drag his left leg throughout his life). Scarcely a work of Szymanowski's middle period passes by without some major reference to the dance. The *Love Songs of Hafiz*, *Mythes*, *Nocturne and Tarantella* for violin and piano, *Métopes*, *Masques*, the Third Symphony and First Violin Concerto, the uncompleted cantata *Agave* (based on Euripides' *Bacchae*), the *Songs of a Fairy Princess*, *Songs of an Infatuated Muezzin* – all contain dance-stylisations, generally of an oriental character. The climax of this phase is undoubtedly the monumental dance-song in Act II of *King Roger* in which the shepherd effectively bewitches Roger's entire court.

Apropos this part of *King Roger*, Szymanowski wrote in a letter to a friend: 'Concerning the theme of the dance, about which you ask, it is *absolutely my patent*. I am delighted that I so succeeded in counterfeiting its "authenticity" that you felt obliged to search out truly "authentic" sources for verification.' He goes on to make a disparaging reference to the pseudo-orientalism of Rimsky-Korsakov and his followers, overlooking the fact that, essentially, his own exotic stylisations are derived from the Franco-Russian tradition which began with Rimsky-Korsakov and Borodin, gathered momentum with Debussy and Ravel (the overall indebtedness of the *Prélude à l'Après-Midi d'un Faune* to *Antar* tends to be overlooked) and reached its *ne plus ultra* in the works of Florent Schmitt, Dukas' *La Péri* and early Stravinsky. This was the *donnée*, but Szymanowski treated and personalised it in a way which reflects not only his fastidiousness but his first-hand knowledge and love of the East. He associated with like-minded men. Jarosław Iwaszkiewicz, the poet, playwright and novelist,[1] was a cousin and lifelong friend whose interest in the East was expressed in such works as *Escape to Baghdad* and in the poems which Szymanowski set in 1918 as *Songs of an Infatuated Muezzin*. Iwaszkiewicz was fascinated by the interaction of Arabic, Greek and European cultures, particularly by the fraught relationship between classical paganism and Christianity; in later years he wrote a book on Sicily and its history. In all respects, therefore, he was eminently qualified as the librettist for *King Roger*. He also made the Polish translations of texts by other poets set by Szymanowski, including the *Tagore Songs*, Op. 41, and the four Joyce settings of Op. 54. He published an account of his friendship with the composer in 1947 and a study of *Harnasie* in 1964.

Then there was Tadeusz Miciński, poet of the Four Songs, Op. 11, the Six Songs, Op. 20, and the inspirational force behind the *Concert Overture* and the First Violin Concerto. He was steeped in Eastern culture and religion and profoundly influenced by them in his own esoteric and mystical beliefs. Miciński made the Polish version of the poem by the thirteenth-century Islamic poet Jalal'ad-Din Rumi which inspired the Third Symphony, *The Song of the Night*. Oriental poetry itself, however, Szymanowski first discovered in the form of translations of Hafiz by Hans Bethge, whose exquisite renderings of Li-Tai-Po are set to music in Mahler's *Das Lied von der Erde*. Another interesting coincidence in this context is that Friedrich Rückert, author of the *Kindertotenlieder*, was also one of the earliest German translators of Rumi. The appeal to ravaged and world-weary

[1] He is probably best known to the English for his play *Summer in Nohant* about Chopin and Georges Sand.

Western sensibilities of immemorial oriental verse, with its clear, spare textures and vein of philosophic detachment, is not hard to understand; of a similar vintage is Zemlinsky's *Lyric Symphony* of 1922–3, seven linked settings of poems drawn from Hans Effenberger's[1] German translations of Tagore's *The Gardener* (several of which had already been set by Szymanowski in his Op. 41).

Though Szymanowski's knowledge of the culture and history of the Arab world was extensive, and was put to excellent use in *King Roger*, there is little evidence to suggest that he ever took more than a casual interest in authentic Arab music. Once Bartók had determined ethnic music to be his vocation he found little difficulty in casting off uncongenial fetters. Szymanowski's roots were too firmly embedded in Western culture for him to do this. He was, and remained at heart, a 'good European'. We shall see, however, that, like Skryabin, he approached on occasion the true *matter* of Eastern music as opposed to its stylised, Europeanised *manner*; this came about, quite spontaneously, because the nature of his poetic thought demanded it.

Szymanowski's contact with oriental and classical antiquity engendered a species of spiritual and aesthetic awakening, a quickened perception, an urge to be made perfect by the love of visible beauty. So it was that his music became more and more a matter of beauty of sound; of sounds which, exquisitely arranged and glorious to the ear, suggest wonderful and indefinable impressions far removed from the domain of the abstract and intellectual. Impressionism in music is above all a sensuous art, the secret of suggestion, of causing delicious sensations by the use of sounds. The First Violin Concerto is nominally a transmutation into music of some blank verse of Miciński, the Third Symphony a setting of Jalal'ad-Din Rumi; yet in a sense they are two of the most perfect pieces of 'pure' music in existence, since every sound and phrase and line is sonorous, ringing and echoing with 'music' in the poetic sense. In bringing to life this *vie intérieure* or 'inscape' Szymanowski stakes his claim to be considered not only one of Poland's finest artists but one of the twentieth century's best composers. It is significant that after the Second Symphony he never again returned to the genre in its traditional guise, however frequently he may have diverted the

---

[1] Otherwise known as Jan Effenberg-Sliwiński or simply as Jan Sliwiński, he was an ardent and lifelong propagandist for Polish culture, particularly for Szymanowski's music. He translated many of the composer's Polish song-texts into German.

outlines of first-movement sonata form to his own ends. The dynamic cut and thrust of 'development' was alien to his sensibility, which revealed itself now as too inward-looking, too contemplative, too involved with its own sensations and nervous responses, to encompass the energetic, rhetorical, dynamic 'imperialism' endemic in symphonic utterance. His music needed merely to *be*, not to *become*. No wonder, then, that he recoiled from the harsh glare of German romanticism in favour of the mists and half-lights of French Impressionism, of Debussy, whose concern, orientally passive (but in a positive sense), was for the intrinsic, superhuman beauty of 'mere things' when isolated from their utilitarian (i.e. symphonic or dialectic) context and rendered as they are, in and for themselves. Such men experience an absolute congruence, or harmony, between the world of matter and that of the spirit; and indeed it is no accident that in the work of the great twentieth-century poets-in-music – Delius, Debussy, Ravel, Szymanowski, Messiaen – *harmony* (in the musical sense) is a matter of vital concern.

Yet for all that the Impressionist aesthetic now comes to play a role of paramount importance in the evolution of Szymanowski's characteristic style; it *complements* rather than conflicts with, *enhances* rather than displaces, the romantic elements which have already taken root there. Familiar Impressionist preoccupations are well in evidence – night (First Violin Concerto, Third Symphony, Act II of *King Roger*), water (*Mythes, Métopes*), the exotic in the form either of the East (*Love Songs of Hafiz, Songs of an Infatuated Muezzin*, the Third Symphony and *King Roger* again) or of classical antiquity (*Mythes, Métopes*, the cantata *Demeter*). Szymanowski's discovery of Debussy and Ravel was of course a crucial factor here; but we should not leave out of account a composer, practically forgotten today, who made in his work a special synthesis of Impressionist and German-romantic elements which caused no small stir at the time, namely Franz Schreker (1878–1934). Szymanowski was present at the 1913 production in Vienna of his opera *Das Spielwerk und die Prinzessin* (it was around the same time in the same place that he first encountered *Pelléas et Mélisande* and *Petrushka*), and in 1928, on the occasion of Schreker's fiftieth birthday, paid him tribute in an article he contributed to *Musikblätter des Anbruch*. *King Roger* in particular suggests that Schreker's *Der ferne Klang* had left its mark, as it did on Erich Wolfgang Korngold's early operas (*Violanta, Die tote Stadt*) and on Weinberger's *Schwanda the Bagpiper*. Like Schreker, Szymanowski found himself drawn to widening the harmonic orbit of Impressionism (in common with Delius, Debussy and Ravel he habitually composed at the piano, 'without which', claimed the latter, 'you can't invent new harmonies'). One of the reasons that the first of the *Mythes*, 'La Fontaine d'Aréthuse', became more popular than its companions was probably that its harmonic idiom is less advanced – far less so, certainly, than that of the *Métopes* and *Masques*. Yet Szymanowski was too much of an artist-in-sound, too much of a hedonist, ever to abandon himself to indiscriminate dissonance. His discords invariably have a bitonal base: their component parts, however elaborated or diffused, can generally be analysed in terms of two concords sounded simultaneously. He would have agreed with Milhaud who, overwhelmed by the beauty of the opening bar of Roussel's *Pour une Fête de Printemps*, claimed that a polytonal chord is 'more subtly sweet and more violently potent' than a 'normal' one. Certainly much of the sweetness and potency of *King Roger* is a matter of the subtle violence of its harmonic language.

But a German artist – and that is what Szymanowski was by training – naturally tends more to line than to colour, to counterpoint rather than harmony; and it can persuasively be argued that counterpoint (better, *polyphony*) is the backbone of Szymanowski's music. He was first and foremost a linear or melodic or lyrical composer, and this results, in his 'impressionist' period, in a tangible firmness of outline. He is rather like a master of noble metalwork who has divined the secret of manipulating the tenacious bronze or gold into fantastically delicate shapes and patterns. His textures pose great problems for conductors (and recording producers), with such a profusion and intricacy of detail, such a wealth of divergently proliferating lines all clamouring for attention; the difficulty is to know which to select as the most important. Certainly no one could describe Szymanowski's mind or his music as simple or unsophisticated. It is no doubt possible on a first or superficial hearing of the latter to find in it some of the symptoms described by Nietzsche as heralding the end of a civilisation or cultural cycle – the disproportionate importance of detail in relation to design, elaboration for elaboration's sake. But no student of Szymanowski can fail to be struck at a very early stage by his absolute *mastery* of design – another legacy from his prentice period. His instinct for imparting natural form and coherence to the content of his thought is infallible – the First Violin Concerto is his outstanding achievement in this regard – and elsewhere he is adept at ringing his own idiosyncratic changes on many a received formal notion. As for 'elaboration for elaboration's sake', this is all part of a passive and non-Western stance and must be perceived non-Westernly. His superabundant richness of decorative invention and uncanny feeling for evocative piano and orchestral sonorities float will-less (if not regardless), negating the sense of time; the arabesques, the filigrees and the endless iridescent play of colours are all symbols not of narcissistic self-indulgence (as in the totally 'Western' complexity and elaboration of Reger's work, for example) but of ecstasy, of intoxication.

One final point relating to the matter of Szymanowski's 'decadence' can be made if we compare works like the Third Symphony or First String Quartet, which employ Wagnerian phraseology and texture, with a piece like Zemlinsky's *Lyric Symphony* which is stylistically somewhat compatible. In musical terms 'decadence' means above all the protracting of the cadence or cadential feeling to vast proportions, and the *Lyric Symphony* does just this: like *Das Lied von der Erde* (on which it was partially modelled) it is a large-scale song of farewell. Delius, Elgar and Rachmaninov no less than Mahler, Korngold and Zemlinsky all luxuriate in this sunset sensation, this 'sinking feeling'; but Szymanowski hardly at all.

Not only French but Russian music in the form of Skryabin (already as we have seen an early enthusiasm) played a significant and fascinating role in the liberating process, for the special type of *ecstasis* to which he aspired is frequently to be encountered in Szymanowski. In fact, the vein of ecstatic languor, sensuousness or even sensuality, which pervades Szymanowski's music in some degree of *all* periods is of unmistakable Skryabinic provenance, and Szymanowski's use of the solo violin to give expression to this type of feeling in many works is almost certainly a legacy from the *Poem of Ecstasy*. The Russian connection was a natural outcome of Szymanowski's anti-Germanism, but Skryabin is the only composer to leave a definite personal impress. Piano sonorities in *Mythes*, *Métopes* and *Masques* are frequently Skryabin-derived: motivic molecules crowd together to form exquisite patterns (like Chladni's plate), and tremolos and trills are employed for their intrinsic quality as *timbre*, as a musical Impressionist translation of shimmering heat or light. Furthermore, Skryabin's knowledge of Hindu mysticism led inevitably to the appearance of certain oriental traits in his music. The Impressionist concept of sounds or textures as *objets sonores* is itself Eastern in character, since the Buddhist does his perceiving in terms of intensity of existence, profundity of significance, relationships within a pattern; he is not concerned with spatial or temporal categories. Hence certain characteristics of the mature Skryabin which are perpetuated and developed in Szymanowski. '*Instead of the dynamic, functional flow of traditional music, Skryabin explores the possibility of musical stasis, equivalent to an imaginary paradise of the sense beyond time*. . . . This is no less obvious when the music *seems* to have mobility and pulse.'[1]

Faubian Bowers relates Skryabin's disdain for chronological time to the type of disorientation achieved by drugs. Henry Miller wrote in *Nexus*: '*Poème de l'Extase* . . . it was like a bath of ice; cocaine and rainbows. For weeks I went about in a trance . . . the divine Skryabin.' In the same work, young listeners now find a species of psychedelic exaltation, and there can be no doubt that, in his quasi-religious urge to transcend self-conscious selfhood, Skryabin's fantasies can be allied in their effect with such well-known chemical surrogates of religion as alcohol, pot, LSD and many other *poisons sacrés*. Alistair Wightman has raised this matter in connection with the works of Szymanowski's middle years. Noting that a small amount of cocaine was found on the composer after his death, Wightman points out that in his Zakopane days Szymanowski was a close friend of the painter and dramatist Stanislaw Witkiewicz, who experimented with drugs as he worked. To Wightman, 'certain features seem to be drug-inspired . . . the high, floating, almost disembodied lines, the extremely vivid, colouristic use of the orchestra'.

The few fragments which have survived of Szymanowski's two-volume novel *Ephebos* strongly suggest what Huxley called 'the mind's antipodes', areas of consciousness visited only in a state of preternatural exaltation. This work in fact was written in 1918–19 as a result of a most pressing need to escape from reality. The Russian Revolution had broken out in 1917 and Tymoszówka was destroyed. Szymanowski found himself stranded in sordid circumstances in Elisavetgrad with death, violence and crime all part of the day's routine. Composition came almost to a standstill; instead there rose 'a magic vision of Italy before the mind's eye' in the form of *Ephebos*, 'a sweet remembrance of things past . . . an assertion of the Omnipotent Beauty of life even in the midst of suffering'. These

[1] Hugh Macdonald, *Skryabin* (Oxford Studies of Composers, London.) My italics.

words come from the introduction; here, published in English translation for the first time, is one of the few fragments of the text to have escaped destruction in Warsaw in 1939:

. . . Basileus sent them to the distant capital Panormos on his speedy ship, that they might adorn with their art the new Temple of the Holy Mother, built to honour Her by Admiral Georgius Antiochenos, commander of the unconquered fleet of Roger II, King of the Normans and of both Sicilies.

Half awake, half dreaming, Enoch Porfir stands leaning against the great mast. At the top of the mast blows the claret-coloured flag of the Caesars bearing a wreathed cross at its centre. His whole life suddenly becomes a wonder, a long-forgotten myth, an enchanting fable: one of those which in happy childhood he heard, by the green banks of the rapid waters of the Alpheus, from the lips – the lips of someone whose name he cannot even remember, but with whom he strolled through green groves, emerald hilly slopes, inaccessible crevices and gorges fragrant with absinth and thyme.

What was it like? . . . Memory fades in the dusk of the past: certain scents; shimmering lights; the sounds of long-forgotten words; distant reminiscences like dappled butterflies all circling around the youth's head. His eyes sink into the deep sapphire waters. Above his head the wind sings in the giant swollen sails. The iron joints of the ship's body grate and whine in lament. Further and further away lie – burning and glowing in the setting sun, piled up and bundled together, monstrous and magnificent in their chaos – the stone walls, golden domes and swift, slender spires of the terrible city of Byzantium. Over there the huge, swollen domes of the Hagia Sophia in which the sun has lit a blinding purple flame; there on the hills stand ranks of cypress, black, as if chiselled out of labradorite; a little further, the cupola of the church of Miriamdrion, then the grey walls of the temple of the Saviour Mone-tes-Choras, and beyond the enchanting apse of the Hyperagia Theotokos, supported by slender columns. Next the Chalcedonian Steps, leading to the port, where stands the Golden Gate through which the triumphant Caesars, at the head of their legions, so often entered the city. Further still the haughty bastions and turrets of Fort Bucoleont, then the massive marble walls of the Hippodrome and the alcoves of the walls of the Golden Palace of the Basils, concealing within themselves so many cruel crimes, that had drowned in blood the marvellous green marble – *verde antico* – the white Phrygian red-veined marble; the Pentelicon reddened by the morning sun; the Thessalian blue-green; the pink onyx and finally the scarlet porfir; all adorning those chambers out of which were born so many generations of Cosmokrats, the Porfirogents, the rulers of the world. And at the centre of the vaulted ceiling, surrounded by golden stars, the emerald mosaic cross gently glitters.

Deep in thought Porfir watched the day dying with the sun above the huge city – a day that stuck out like a signpost at the crossroads of his life. Slowly the lights dimmed and the sounds of the city grew faint. The sleepy silence floated in a vast silence of invisible, immeasurable waters. . . . The ship heaved smoothly and swiftly through the gently splashing waves. Passing by was the outline of the islands of Prinkipos, fragrant with trees and flowers heated by the glow of the day's sun.

Soon the green distant banks of Propontyd will come together, and at dawn – through the narrow corridor of Hellespont – they will reach the high sea. Fantasy begins to take wing. Stirred by hidden emotions, Porfir's heart flaps like a bird in a cage. As the stars come out, long-extinguished memories from childhood are lit up in his consciousness. The sleepy, rhythmic hiss of the waves softly striking the hull of the ship is like the whispering of intimate words about long-forgotten matters. The stars: a golden mosaic on the heavenly dome, sparkling, dappled and distant . . . floating into an uncharted abyss, silvery with dreamy longings of the Milky Way. . . .[1]

Little attention needs to be drawn to the prevailing hothouse influences here of writers like Wilde, Huysmans and Pater (a kind of enriched *Marius the Epicurean*); but the most striking affinity is with an English writer of the same so-called 'decadent' period, Arthur Machen (presumably unknown to Szymanowski). The hero of Machen's masterpiece, *The Hill of Dreams*, similarly finds the day-to-day world so intolerably burdensome that, like Szymanowski, he retreats into the fantasy-land of classical antiquity, rebuilding in his mind the splendid and golden city of Roman Siluria; set in the midst of this New Jerusalem was the garden of Avallaunius, which is of course Eden, the garden of primal innocence, to which Szymanowski in all his music of this period aspires.

It is recorded that Ananda, the beloved disciple of Buddha, once saluted his master and said 'Half the holy life, O master, is friendship with the beautiful, association with the beautiful, communion with the beautiful.' Whereupon the master replied: 'Say not so, Ananda, say not so! It is not half of the holy life. It is the whole of the holy life.' This is very well; but in practical terms the cult of 'pure' beauty in music has certain drawbacks. For one thing such music is inordinately dependent on the mechanics of performance – on musicianship and sympathy of insight as well as technical competence in the players, and on extra-musical factors such as acoustic conditions.

Some interesting light is shed on this aspect of Szymanowski's work if we consider the question of its representation on record. So far few record companies in England and America have shown interest in him. Most listeners, like myself, will have come to know the composer almost exclusively through the medium of Polish recordings. While in most cases the quality of performance cannot be impugned, the recorded sound itself leaves much to be desired, a factor which can be overlooked much less readily in Szymanowski's

[1] Translated by Sylvia and Benjamin Shoshan.

case than (say) in Brahms's; even in the newest recordings, such as those of *Harnasie*, the balance tends to be very fierce and close, *King Roger* being a particularly sorry casualty in this respect. Nor is the multi-microphone technique of recording, with its often merciless dissection of detail, necessarily well suited to Szymanowski's scores; a sense of *distance* is always part of the magic of Impressionism, and individual parts matter only in relation to the sum-total. (Imagine trying to isolate a 'detail' of an Impressionist painting!) For this reason the digital process, which uses only a limited number of microphones and permits of no artificial 'mixing' in the control room, is ideal: the gain in perspective afforded by the 'natural' balance, together with a much increased refinement of sound, can be experienced in a revelatory way in Antal Dorati's Decca recording of the Third Symphony, much as one may prefer Witold Rowicki's interpretation.

Not only performers are beset by the inimical power of Beauty. Here is Kaikhosru Sorabji writing of Szymanowski's Third Symphony:

Szymanowski has taken a poem celebrating the beauty, the enigmatic and transcendental beauty of an Eastern night, the like of which is to be found perhaps nowhere in Europe except in Sicily,[1] which belongs as much to the East as it does to the West. Around this poem he has written music of a radiant purity of spirit, of an elevated ecstasy of expression, music so permeated with the very essence of the choicest and rarest specimens of Iranian art – the whole score glows with gorgeous colour, rich, yet never garish nor crude, like a Persian painting or silk rug – that such a feat is unparalleled in Western music. . . .

Evidently the work had a similar effect on Lutoslawski who recalled that he felt quite dizzy for a number of weeks after hearing it.

Now this is the language not merely of admiration but of infatuation, of love-passion. It is beauty which fires the writer with this passion, its object being not a person but music; and the effect is intoxicating, confounding, overwhelming. But no one, neither a composer nor his audience, can live for ever in a state of rapture; it would end by consuming them utterly. Debussy, Delius and Szymanowski, all composers fervently dedicated to the ideal of beauty-in-sound, all faced this problem in middle life, when the ageing process inevitably brings some deadening of perception,

---

[1] Which is very likely whence Szymanowski drew his inspiration for the work, since he never visited Iran.

some touch of frost to the imaginative life. Szymanowski's Beatific Vision, his Great Noontide of creativity, lasted for approximately four years, which coincided with those of the Great War: a time when reality was fit to be and in practical terms *could* be retreated from. With the coming of the Revolution, however, the dream-idyll was over. It is difficult to know to what extent the course of an artist's inner development is affected or indeed determined by extraneous circumstances and events, but it is tempting to see in the newly classical, 'abstract' tendencies of the Third Piano Sonata, the Twelve Studies and the First String Quartet signs that the well-springs of Impressionist inspiration were beginning to dry up anyway. Fired with nationalist ardour following Poland's declaration of independence shortly after the armistice, Szymanowski quickly became aware that, as Poland's most distinguished living composer, some kind of guidance would need to be forthcoming from his direction.

In May 1921, on his way back from his first American trip, he renewed an earlier acquaintance with Stravinsky, whom he heard play part of *Les Noces*; this work, and *Le Sacre du Printemps* which he now came to know for the first time, showed him the possibilities inherent in a realistic, non-sentimental use of folk materials. Through the music not only of Stravinsky but also of Bartók, he saw how it was possible to preserve the primitive and even barbaric elements of folksong and dance in a modern, non-academic but still tonal idiom. Szymanowski found his salvation in the folk music of the Tatra mountains, the 'Polish Highlands'; the *Słopiewnie* songs, written in 1921, are the first attempt at putting the new ideas (and ideals) into practice. In many ways these did not, as might at first sight be supposed, run counter to any of his earlier stylistic inclinations, even had the *Variations on a Polish Theme*, Op. 10, not revealed an embryonic interest in folksong. He had always been a lyrical composer; and the part played by folk music – particularly that of the East – in the development of musical Impressionism is frequently overlooked (folksong and folk-instruments discovered new, or rather very old, pentatonic and modal scalic patterns which brought something akin to the *plein air* of Impressionism in terms both of melody and the harmony implicit in the melody).

As we have seen, the music of Szymanowski's second period was already heavily impregnated with folk-music elements, even though they derived from Arab and Hindu rather than Polish sources. Andrzej Panufnik has surmised that this was due to a hidden atavistic impulse: Bartók was one authority who supported the idea that Slavonic music is of Arabic origin, 'so it is quite possible that Szymanowski, as a Slav, was unconsciously searching for prehistoric elements in Polish folk music – elements which he was eventually to discover at the end of his life'.[1] When we remember too that folk music consists basically of song and dance – as we know, two of the pre-eminent motive forces in Szymanowski's music during his second period – the new turn of development seems even more logical. *Harnasie*, being a ballet with voices, speaks for itself; likewise the *Mazurkas*, Op. 50 and Op. 62, the *Kurpian Songs* (six for unaccompanied chorus and twelve for voice and piano), and the *Four Polish Dances* for piano; and strong folk-dance elements are to be found also in the Second String Quartet, the Second Violin Concerto and the *Symphonie Concertante* for piano and orchestra. *King Roger* was completed during this period (1924) and the outcome of the third act, in which the king recognises, but does not surrender to, the Dionysian within himself, may be regarded as privately symbolic of Szymanowski's stance. So may the strong neo-classical tendencies exhibited in the Third Piano Sonata, both string quartets and the two late concertos, all works whose concentration and economy both of manner and matter contrast strongly with the lavishness and luxury of the romantic-impressionist scores – however skilfully the latter may be contained within a formal framework of concision and density.

From folksong it is but a short step to plainsong – which, like folksong, is modal and non-Western in character – to the music of religion and ritual, to Polish sacred music of the sixteenth century, to the 'atavism' of Szymanowski's *Stabat Mater* and his *Litany to the Virgin Mary*. In the relationship of the Op. 10 *Variations on a Polish Theme* to the Op. 50 *Mazurkas*, the stone which the builder rejected (or at least passed over for many years) eventually became head of the corner. In the same way we can surely find the seeds of the *Stabat Mater* embedded in the Kasprowicz songs, Op. 5, with their Slavic stylisations of peasant religious lamentation, and in the self-conscious 'archaisms' of Act I of *King Roger*. This phenomenon of continuity in disparity serves to attest both the worth and integrity of Szymanowski as an artist, and the age-old truth that music is an art in

---

[1] In an article contributed to the programme booklet for the 1975 London première of *King Roger* at the Coliseum.

flux, for ever returning to its sources to replenish the energies spent in the pursuit of novelty.

Chronological Survey

1909–10: SECOND SYMPHONY

In 1911–12 a concert programme consisting of Szymanowski's Second Symphony conducted by Fitelberg and Second Piano Sonata played by Rubinstein, was given in Berlin, Leipzig and Vienna. This constituted Szymanowski's first important exposure to musical Europe, and by and large made a favourable impression, particularly in Vienna where he was acclaimed by the influential critic Richard Specht. Up to a certain point the two works complement each other. Both contain first movements in classical sonata form; a second movement consisting of a theme and variations, among the latter a gavotte and minuet; and, linked to it, a fugal finale. There, however, the similarity ends. The brawny Teutonic hand of Reger (and refracted through him Beethoven and Brahms) lies so heavily on every aspect of the Sonata that hardly anything of the composer's own personality is permitted to emerge; there is little thematic distinction and even less beauty of texture, particularly in view of Szymanowski's unaccountable fondness for one of Reger's most disagreeable pianistic traits: tightly bunched chords at the extremes of the keyboard. Arguably the best part of the Sonata is the concluding fugue, the progress of which Szymanowski imbues with the same feeling of momentousness, of cumulative excitement bordering on ecstasy, that is to be found in its Regerian prototypes and, indeed, in Szymanowski's other essays in the medium, the Second Symphony and Third Piano Sonata. As Charles Koechlin once said, virtually anyone can write a fugue; the difficulty is to make music out of it. This was no difficulty for Szymanowski.

But if the Second Sonata scarcely sounds authentically Szymanowskian at all, the first movement of the Second Symphony, for all its echoes of Skryabin and Strauss, is quite audibly the progenitor of the First Violin Concerto, which inhabits a similarly ecstatic emotional world. In fact the mouthpiece of the main theme – very typical of Szymanowski-through-Skryabin in its winged lyricism – is none other than the solo violin; even in 1910 it was hardly conventional to begin a symphony with a violin solo:

Ex.2 Symphony No.2

Merely a few bars are sufficient to locate us in the steamy sensualism of *Tristan*, the language of which came into being in the service of sex and sensuality and which is an all-conditioning presence in much of Szymanowski's work. An orchestral symptom of this sensuality, in the first movement of the Symphony, is the recurrent use of the harp *glissando* which often sweeps in crinolined voluptuousness through two bars consecutively.

Although the Symphony as a whole seems designed to show off the composer's prowess as a contrapuntalist, it is significant that Ex. 2, in terms of Szymanowski's own style the most forward-looking of the first movement's three themes, is the one which lends itself the least happily to the laboured and tortuous contrapuntal manoeuvrings to which it is submitted in the development. Like Blake's cherubim, Ex. 2 is the kind of theme which is quite happy just to 'be'; it does not want to 'do' or 'become' anything. In the second movement it undergoes variation or metamorphosis, a quite different process: the leopard may change its spots but remains the same animal underneath. This is why composers who involve themselves with folksong (as Szymanowski later did) are more inclined to write variations than symphonies, for a folksong by its very nature is a fixed entity and cannot grow or evolve or 'become' something else. The climax of the development section (repeated and expanded in the recapitulation) is underpinned by a long pedal-point, a 'fingerprint' of the mature Szymanowski.

The second movement, in which Reger is once again invoked, is a variations and fugue; the latter is virtually a self-contained movement with its own introduction, while the variations embrace both slow movement and scherzo. The scherzo itself is a tripartite structure based not only on the variation theme but also on Ex. 2; in fact the composer here embarks on a *tour de force* of thematic integration and continuity which has no parallel in his *oeuvre*. When the fugue arrives (its model probably the fugal finale of Strauss's *Sinfonia Domestica*), every one of its five subjects prove to be derived from earlier themes. Moreover, in presenting these themes in a quasi-uniform rhythmic and melodic formation – all, as it were, reduced to a basic common denominator – Szymanowski discloses an almost incestuous complexity of interrelationships between them. There ensues a kind of frenzied saturnalia of counterpoint, a Dionysian orgy of a fugue. Only once more, in the finale of the Third Piano Sonata, did he essay such a virtuoso display; it was as though, having shown the world what he was capable of as an artisan, he felt free to pursue his rightful direction as an artist – which led him out of the immediate orbit of German romanticism.

Szymanowski and Fitelberg together revised the scoring of the Symphony in the 1930s. The horns are still expected frequently to scale heights deemed by Norman Del Mar to be 'unfit for human habitation', but this was a Straussian legacy that persisted to the end. Elsewhere Szymanowski may actually have pruned to excess: his disinclination to reinforce important melodic strands by doubling is of less consequence in his later work, which is less self-consciously contrapuntal, but in the first movement of the Second Symphony it means that much passes us by with little hope of being heard. Fitelberg's recording, which presumably represents the composer's intentions, makes clear that the marking 'Allegro moderato, grazioso' at the head of this first movement means simply that the music should *move*, not that it should move *fast*; a hurried tempo is fatally injurious to the rapt mood of the opening.

1911–14: LOVE SONGS OF HAFIZ, OP. 24 AND OP. 26

Hafiz of Shiraz was a fourteenth-century Iranian poet whose sensibility was in many respects akin to Szymanowski's own. He had the pure lyric gift, refined, sensuous and aromatic. He was not a mystic, like Rumi, nor is his hedonism tainted by the pessimism and cynicism of Omar Khayyám; rather does he celebrate spring, roses, wine and love as spiritual, God-given, ecstatic delights in themselves. 'Wine', Huxley shrewdly suggested in *The Doors of Perception*, 'is the Persian's Impressionism,' an interesting analogy from our point of view inasmuch as the oncoming of Szymanowski's Impressionism was patently accelerated by his encounter with Hafiz, which took place in 1911, through the medium of Hans Bethge's German paraphrases, in the Imperial Library in Vienna. In the first instance Szymanowski set six for voice and piano, which constitute Op. 24; then in 1914 added five more which, together with nos. 1, 4 and 5 of Op. 24, he orchestrated to form Op. 26.

Back in 1911 Szymanowski was not yet in a position to make any real declaration of stylistic independence, and the music of Op. 24 is still saturated in 'Viennese' chromaticism. Nevertheless, the choice of oriental texts is itself prophetic, as is the music of no. 4, 'Dance'. Ex. 3 shows Szymanowski's favourite dotted dance-rhythm in 3/8 or its compounds, the static bass, implied bitonal harmony, chords used as needle-points of colour or percussion accents, and tiny melodic fragments repeated over and over in the manner of oriental monody – all marking a radical break with 'Viennese' convention.

Ex.3 Dance *(Love-Songs of Hafiz*, Op.24)

In the Op. 26 songs Szymanowski is even further advanced in his new idiom, the exoticism is more pronounced (i.e. the chromaticism

veers from West to East), and the orchestral technique has now
penetrated the impressionist orbit. The very appearance of the score
on the page glitters and shimmers, and the two harps, celesta, piano
and multi-divided strings are to be mandatory colour constituents of
Szymanowski's orchestra for some years to come. 'Your Voice' is
pure sensuous enchantment of a kind not before experienced in
Szymanowski; Bacchus, the god of wine, is tumultuously invoked in
'Drinking Song'; while 'The Grave of Hafiz', arguably the finest
song of the cycle, movingly expresses the contrast between the
remote and frozen immobility of death and the grave and the fresh-
springing, impassioned, life-intoxicated earth which the singer has
left behind for ever. With ironic appropriateness the voice and piano
version of this epitaph was issued only in 1937, shortly after the
composer's death, and was designated 'Op.posth.'

A word on Szymanowski's penchant for songs with orchestra.
The youthful *Penthesilea* was the first, the main interest of which, as
Adam Neuer has pointed out, is its pre-impressionist water-music.
Thereafter Szymanowski orchestrated selected songs, not only from
the Hafiz collection but from the *Songs of a Fairy Princess* in 1933 and
the *Songs of an Infatuated Muezzin* in 1934, in both latter cases many
years after they were originally composed (1915 and 1918 respec-
tively). The *Słopiewnie* of 1921 were orchestrated in 1928 for a small
ensemble. In many ways the instrumental versions of these works
must be regarded as definitive, since the accompaniments are not so
much 'orchestrated' as recomposed in orchestral terms. Since several
of Szymanowski's finest achievements belong in this genre it is a pity
that not a note of them has been recorded, even in Poland.

1915: MYTHES

The three *Mythes*, for violin and piano, were composed at Józef
Jaroszyński's estate Zarudzie between March and June of 1915.
When Szymanowski arrived at Zarudzie he found the Kochańskis
staying there, and it was in close collaboration with Paweł that he
composed not only the *Mythes* but also the two violin concertos.
Szymanowski was always proud to acknowledge the fact of this
collaboration. In a letter to Zofia Kochańska, Paweł's wife and the
dedicatee of the *Mythes*, written many years later in March 1930, he
claimed that he and Paweł together created 'a new style, a new mode
of expression for the violin. . . . All works by other composers

related to this style (no matter how much creative genius they revealed) came later, that is through the direct influence of *Mythes* and the [First] Concerto, or else through direct collaboration with Paweł.'[1] This new style can best be classified as 'impressionistic', and *Mythes* mark the onset of Szymanowski's mature 'impressionist' period. For, as in the case of Debussy's harmony, few of the techniques he employed in these violin works – extensive double-stopping, tremolandos, harmonics, triple and quadruple *pizzicato*, simultaneous arco and left-hand pizzicato, the *sul ponticello*, chains of trills, the notated *glissando*, even the quarter-tones – were new in themselves. What *was* new was the manner and spirit in which they were employed, i.e. in the exploration of timbre *per se* rather than in the service of virtuoso display. Szymanowski removes the element of self-consciousness from virtuosity: the technical devices are not 'featured', but are simply the means for the composer to say what he has to say. The same purely artistic, poetic impulse fuses violin and piano as a single entity, an indivisible sound-complex; the pianist must be no mere professional accompanist but as fine and skilled a musician in his own right as the violinist.[2]

That this poses practical problems can be clearly heard if one listens to the various recordings of *Mythes* made over the years: only those in which the pianist is himself an artist of the first rank are really successful, and it is hard to imagine the Deutsche Grammophon issue with Kaja Danczowska and Krystian Zimerman being readily outclassed. The very opening of the first and most celebrated of the *Mythes*, 'La Fontaine d'Aréthuse', provides a measure of the difficulties. The piece opens with a magical shimmer of piano sonority (Ex. 4). The sky is deep azure; the strong southern sunlight pours down in a flood; the sound of the water as it plashes and rings in the fountain is heard as if through a quivering heat-haze. This sheen or spray of bitonal sound needs the most sensitively calculated balance and shading if it is not to emerge as a mere jangle.

[1] See A. Wightman 'Szymanowski, Bartók and the violin', *Musical Times*, March 1981.

[2] The PWM/Universal Complete Edition of the works for violin and piano (Vol. 9) draws attention to the fact that Szymanowski occasionally elaborated the printed piano parts in performance; at certain points in 'La Fontaine d'Aréthuse' he created a special atmospheric effect by depressing silently the notes of the chord that had first been sounded and then changing the pedal.

The writing for both instruments in Szymanowski's single earlier extended work for violin and piano, the 1904 Violin Sonata, Op. 9, had been dull and conventional, as indeed had its substance. But in 'La Fontaine d'Aréthuse' there is now no mistaking the composer's

Ex.4 La Fontaine d'Aréthuse *(Mythes)*

(a)

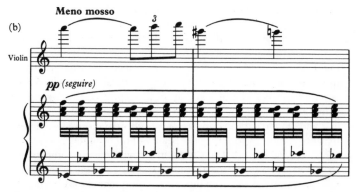

identity. In it Szymanowski achieves for the first time the successful and utterly personal cross-fertilisation between romantic lyricism and atmospheric impressionism to which the First Violin Concerto and the Third Symphony, *Le Chant de la Nuit*, owe a large measure of their glory. He reveals himself as a true poet-in-sound, one moreover whose quasi-rhapsodic spontaneity of expression belies the music's strong structural foundations. The freedom is paradoxically contained *within* the discipline of the writing; fantasy dictates forms of which ornamentation is an integral part, not a surface encrustation.

If we chart the course of 'La Fontaine d'Aréthuse', we find to begin with that the first important 'theme' is not a melody but a continuous, quasi-immobile texture – Ex. 4a, the *Jeux d'eau* of the fountain which ripple and foam in a fluid 7/8 metre (two bars of 2/8 followed by one of 3/8). Its restricted compass ensures that when, later on, after the violin's ethereal entry with its finely moulded, orientally inflected melody (Ex. 4b), deep resonant bass notes and glancing *staccato* octaves in the extreme upper register make their appearance, the effect is of a wonderfully subtle broadening of the sound-spectrum. The violin melody, gaining confidence, now comes gradually to dominate the scene in a gloriously passionate outburst (*molto espressivo ed affettuoso*) which contrasts notably with the shimmering void out of which it originally emerged. A short *molto agitato* central section leads to the return of the fountain music, but this time the violin sings its song two octaves lower, interpolates cadenzas and, in the coda, becomes entranced by the lower (black-note) voice of the ostinato, previously the exclusive prerogative of the piano (see Ex. 4, left hand).

'La Fontaine d'Aréthuse' is a mood-piece. 'Narcisse', the 'slow movement' of the triptych, is more a narrative, its subject being the story of Narcissus who fell in love with his own reflection in a pool and was turned into a flower. Expectedly, the lyrical, melodic element is more pronounced and sustained in this miniature symphonic poem than in 'La Fontaine d'Aréthuse', and if the notion of sonata form is to be invoked at all in respect of the *Mythes*, we certainly find here two well-defined thematic entities corresponding to first and second subjects, and a tranquil chordal motif which surely represents Narcissus admiring the beauty of his own reflection in the water. A central episode takes wing in a new thematic complex and Szymanowski draws all the threads together (including the quasi-static still-water chords) in an intense and eloquent climax during the course of which themes not only combine contrapuntally but, at one point, urge violin and piano to enter into strenuous canonic competition with each other. The note of yearning and pathos is maintained in a coda which muses in its brief wilting span over fragments of all the themes and expires pathetically on an incomplete statement of Narcissus' own.

The last piece, 'Dryades et Pan', is a *scherzo fantastique*, its structure determined in all respects by the underlying quasi-balletic scenario which, unlike 'Narcisse', can be quite easily deduced from the music. In the introduction a hot summer wind blows through the forest, causing it to tremor and quiver into activity, the combination of quarter-tones and semitones in the orbit of the violin's open D-string creating an effect as of some nasal oriental reed instrument:

Ex.5 Dryades et Pan *(Mythes)*

The Dryads' dance begins, gathering momentum through ecstatic trills, flashing and flashy arabesques, and vertiginously slithering sequences of double-stopped major seconds. It abruptly breaks off when the sound of Pan's flute is heard on the hills (unaccompanied violin cadenza in harmonics). Now Pan performs a long solo dance, languidly at first, playing his flute the while; little by little he exerts his power in increasingly chromatic contortions of his theme and wild, ululating glissandos in both single and double notes. The ultimate effect is to rouse the Dryads to a resumption of their own orgiastic dance; but now of course the god is both leader and participant and their two themes mingle in increasingly promiscuous, lascivious counterpoint until a climax of Pan-ic ecstasy is reached and the dancers fall exhausted to the ground. In the coda Pan picks up his flute and departs; the forest murmurs die away into silence; and the last sound is that of the Pan-pipes heard as if from the far distance.

1915: SONGS OF A FAIRY PRINCESS

Songs of a Fairy Princess, for coloratura soprano and piano, was something of a Szymanowski family affair. They were inscribed to his sister Stasia (known professionally as Stanislawa Korwin-Szymanowska) who had a fine soprano voice and often took part in recitals and first performances of his works. The original poems in Polish and their French version were the work of Szymanowski's other sister, Zofia. The use of the coloratura with its many high-range trills, quasi-oriental melismas and cadenzas is explained in the second song, 'The Nightingale': the princess advises us that God has put a nightingale in her breast in place of a heart. The entire cycle, therefore, is a *Chant du Rossignol* (the many references to Stravinsky's opera cannot be fortuitous[1]) and, inasmuch as nightingales sing at night, for the greater part of its duration a *Chant de la Nuit* as well. The last song, 'The Feast', is the finest. A feast is in progress in the palace and a rowdy, dissolutely dissonant affair it sounds to be: but the princess flees in pursuit of her lover's wild, free music (another dance) which she can hear from without, and ends her song in trilled ecstatic greeting to the sun and the fields in full bloom. The aura of artificiality is very Ravelian, and the idea of a fairy-tale child-princess singing with the voice of a nightingale would have made an obvious appeal to Ravel.[2] Elsewhere he is recalled, not so much by any

[1] Stravinsky also casts his nightingale as a coloratura soprano. Szymanowski heard the opera in London in June 1914.

[2] Childless men like Ravel and Szymanowski often have a better understanding of and rapport with children than many parents. This is certainly borne out by the *Twenty Children's Rhymes*, Op. 49, which are very much children's adult music as opposed to adults' children's music.

additional 'fingerprints' as by the general brittleness and bitter-sweetness (more bitter than sweet, actually) of the harmonic colouring. Ravelian, too, is the use of the piano (as in *Masques*) to impersonate other instruments – in no. 5 the harp, in no. 6 at first brass fanfares, and then later flute and tambourine (typically, neither of these was included in the three Szymanowski selected for orchestration in 1933).

1915–16: MÉTOPES AND MASQUES

Mythes was the first of the three 'M's, a triptych of triptychs all inspired by 'myths' of one period or another. *Métopes*, like *Mythes*, belongs to the world of Greek mythology: metopes are the square spaces alternating with the triglyphs or grooved tablets in a Doric frieze, and Szymanowski was almost certainly remembering those from the temple of Selinunt in Sicily he had seen in the museum at Palermo. Around the time of the composition of *Mythes* and *Métopes* the composer was immersed in translations of Aeschylus and in Charles Diehl's *Promenades archéologiques en Méditerranée*, and the titles of the three tableaux of *Métopes* – 'L'Ile des Sirènes', 'Calypso' and 'Nausicaa' – originate, of course, in the *Odyssey*. However, the 'humanism' of *Mythes* has disappeared; whereas Szymanowski had brought Arethusa, Narcissus and Pan to warm, vibrant life, these classical evocations are quite lifeless (in a non-pejorative sense) – highly polished, hard and exquisite, essentially cold and remote. They express a temper original, delicate and aristocratic, disdainful of the facile and commonplace, a sensibility often troubled and shadowy and fantastic; but, like the metopes themselves, they are as things transfixed in endless night, icy and phosphorescent. As impressionist sea-music they derive pianistically from Ravel (*Miroirs* and *Gaspard de la Nuit*) rather than from Debussy, despite the generic resemblance to *L'Ile Joyeuse*, the most overtly exotic of all Debussy's sea-pieces; but the 'coldness' is a matter not only of the inherently crystalline quality of piano sonority but also of harmonic texture – the norm of dissonance is much increased, though always on a bitonal basis. Familiar features of pianistic Impressionism abound – watery trills and tremolos; atmospheric use of the pedal to form a haze of sound; fine sprays of arpeggio; voluptuously spread chords; fine threads of melismata and arabesque on the one hand, sonorous climaxes on the other, all spun from the merest motivic fragments.

In 'L'Ile des Sirènes' a two-bar melody must be regarded as the honey-sweet song of the Sirens itself, a song which acquires a kind of narcotic inexorability as it increases in volume and surrounds itself with an ever more glamorous and seductive array of textural ornamentation. A slight element of contrast is provided by a motif in 6/8 marked *dolce scherzando* which returns in the coda, in which the Sirens and all their blandishments are lost in the mist. Their preliminary repertoire is carefully rehearsed in the *Jeux de vagues* of the introduction (marked *molto rubato ed improvisando*), and Jim Samson sees Homeric detail 'in configurations which presumably reflect the double flute and lyre associated . . . with the Sirens. Some of these patterns also suggest bird-calls, reminding us that the Sirens were half-bird and half-woman.' It is difficult not to hear pre-echoes of Messiaen, not only in the *oiseaux exotiques* but also in the percussive character of the dissonance in many passages.

Notably Messiaenic also – certainly very un-Western – is the structure of 'Calypso', which consists of small self-contained units generally no more than a few bars each, not developed but alternated as if at will. Each unit may be extended, curtailed or internally varied, but always *as* a unit, never in a broad paragraph or as part of a line of argument. The main theme *does* make several attempts to grow, but is always interrupted by the return of one of the other units. As a result, despite a couple of *fortissimos*, no really unequivocal climax is ever built up; the effect is precisely that of a metope in a frieze, static and lifeless. Indeed, during the seven years that Ulysses was held captive on Calypso's isle he was scarcely capable of much movement or 'life'; and the music's generally opaque colouring and want of development may suggest something of his frustration and despondence.

By contrast 'Nausicaa' is all air and light and dancing motion. When Ulysses was shipwrecked on the coast of Phaeacia he awoke from a deep sleep to see Nausicaa, daughter of the ruler of the country, leading her handmaidens in a spirited dance. Unlike the Sirens and Calypso, Nausicaa's intentions in Ulysses' regard are entirely honourable: therefore her bitonality is euphonious and innocent-sounding. At the start of the dance the left hand is clearly in D, the right in G sharp minor; yet, remote as they seem to be, the keys complement each other beautifully, and by the time they join together in the very last bar the ear accepts the chord much as it would an ordinary triad. As the dance gathers momentum all maidenly modesty is cast aside, and an accelerando-cum-crescendo (fiendishly difficult to play) culminates in a cascade of arpeggios down the keyboard, white notes against blacks. If this sounds familiar it is because one of the 'units' in 'Calypso' is made up precisely of these ingredients; and, sure enough, the climax of 'Nausicaa' is, in fact, the *fortissimo* return of the main 'Calypso' theme with Nausicaa's neatly joined in counterpoint. How clever! It is a striking gesture, even if one cannot help speculating as to what Szymanowski had in mind in making it; for the paths of Calypso and Nausicaa never crossed, and all they had in common was their attraction to Ulysses. This may be the answer; for a single moment Ulysses is in Nausicaa's power, just as he had been in Calypso's.

The *Métopes* were completed in August 1915 after Szymanowski's return from Zaradzie to Tymoszówka; *Masques* also had been started in the summer of that same year but was not completed until the summer of the next. The title suggests both the *Commedia dell' Arte* and Debussy, neither irrelevantly;[1] for although none of Szymanowski's three characters belong to the pierrot world, the music's general *character* most certainly does: that is, to the kind of ironic perspective in which Debussy so mordantly places this 'world' in the Cello Sonata and elsewhere.[2] In the latter's earlier work – the Verlaine songs, the *Suite Bergamasque* and *Masques* – the nostalgia of the *fêtes galantes* is evoked, as it is in Fauré, more sweetly than bitterly; by the time of the *Etudes* and *En blanc et noir* and the instrumental sonatas the image has been reversed. Similarly there is no innocence of spirit or any true light-heartedness in Szymanowski's *Masques* – for one thing the harmony is even more unrelievedly dissonant than in *Métopes* – and it is perhaps significant that, like Debussy's late Harlequin pieces, they were a product of the war years.

We can surely recognise as an extra ironic dimension the fact that,

---

[1] Skryabin's 'Masque' (singular) – No. 1 of the *Two Poems*, Op. 63 – has no *Commedia dell' Arte* connotations; the title here, like that of its companion piece 'Etrangeté', serves merely to indicate the music's generally enigmatic nature.

[2] Jim Samson, who has examined the score of the unpublished 1920 *Commedia dell' Arte* ballet *Mandragora*, describes its scenario as similar in theme to that of Prokofiev's *Love for Three Oranges*, and remarks, 'Light entertainment it may be, but there are hints too of a more bitter irony in Szymanowski's treatment of the well-known fantasy characters at a time when he himself felt unable to rely on his own inner world of fantasy'. Clearly, therefore, the roots of *Mandragora* are to be found embedded in *Masques*, another instance of Szymanowski's consistency of development.

though Szymanowski chooses three subjects all of which have been depicted by other composers – Sheherazade, Tristan (an anagram of Tantris) and Don Juan – he avoids making any allusion, tongue-in-cheek or otherwise, to their previous musical incarnations. The piano writing is more consistently brilliant than *Métopes*, which probably explains the greater popularity of *Masques*; this despite the fact that some people (among them Rubinstein, the dedicatee of 'Serenade de Don Juan') have felt the music to be conceived essentially in orchestral rather than pianistic terms. Certainly Szymanowski announced his intention of orchestrating *Masques*, which throw off many a cocksure impersonation of orchestral instruments: trumpet fanfares and timpani figures in 'Sheherazade', side drum and xylophone in 'Tantris le Bouffon', the strumming of mandolins and guitars in the 'Sérénade de Don Juan'. But surely this is all part of the 'mask', the illusion, the entertainment. Ravel's 'Alborada del Gracioso' (from *Miroirs*) has been cited as a fairly close stylistic relative of Szymanowski's own jester Tantris;[1] and it is significant that in Ravel's orchestral transcription of 'Alborada' something of the original's biting immediacy is lost. 'Tantris', like 'Alborada', depends much for its resonance on the interplay of different registers within the same sound-box, a phenomenon that no orchestra can satisfactorily simulate. As Messiaen once remarked, 'There exists an orchestral kind of piano writing which is more orchestral than the orchestra itself, and which, with a real orchestra, it is impossible to realise.'

Each of the *Masques* opens with an extensive introduction; thereafter the form is idiosyncratic. That of the first is not unlike 'Dryades et Pan' in *Mythes*. Sheherazade captivates her audience by a slow dance with sinuous, seductive movements which exhales a heady, Skryabinesque perfume; she begins her business in earnest in a lilting 6/8 over a left-hand trill, and a first climax is reached principally through the agency of a motif which lends itself readily enough to frenetic and hammered repetition. After a temporary lull the dance resumes and works to a second climax which is an elaborated and intensified version of the first (a favourite Szymanowskian procedure). The music finally disperses in the Skryabinesque aroma of the introduction, thus completing an arch-form.

[1] Vladimir Janklevitch once described Ravel's 'Gracioso' as 'a kind of Andalusian Petrushka'; and indeed the ghost of Stravinsky's puppet can still be seen 'gesticulating wildly' in the second and third movements of *Masques*.

'Tantris le Bouffon' refers to *Tantris der Narr*, a parody of the Tristan story by Ernst Hardt (1876–1947) published in 1908. Tantris (Tristan) tries one night to steal into Isolde's apartment but is recognised by the dogs and succeeds only in rousing the household. Finally Isolde, naked, is handed over by King Mark to the lepers. Szymanowski does not, alas, portray any of these events in specific detail; rather does he concentrate on the alternation of two moods – the sardonic, and the sentimental bordering on the pathetic. The octaves in a third motif sound in lugubrious remoteness, as if heard through a curtain of water, *englouti*. 'Development' in this case means the subjecting of the first theme to distortion and dismemberment; Szymanowski here moves into the aura of Bartókian or Prokofievian pianistic sadism in which the instrument becomes a transmitter of sound in the raw. Yet he does not mock the demented lover; rather, in a climax which turns the sentimental theme into a fiercely passionate outburst, he engages our sympathy for him.

The 'Sérénade de Don Juan' is basically a rondo, a form ideally suited to the portrayal of an egocentric: as Alistair Wightman has pointed out, the *ritornello* stands for the subject's preoccupation with himself. In this case the build of the *ritornello* itself is symptomatic: the tonic repeats itself narcissistically and never allows the tune to roam far from its starting-point:

Ex.6 Sérénade de Don Juan *(Masques)*

The reiterated D flats start to assert themselves during the preludial cadenza in which the aspiring lover indulges in a particularly exhibitionistic routine of tuning up. The interpolated triplets characteristic of Spanish music form an integral part not only of the *ritornello* itself (see bar 3 of Ex. 6) but also of the many accompanimental patterns which cluster round the tune as it swaggers its way through. The many intimations of a polonaise-type rhythm (which also interpolates triplets) become explicit in the variation marked *pomposo*, which builds itself up grandly, *con forza e passione*, to the main climax. For all the Don's quasi-virtuoso efforts and pretensions, the final chord sounds uncommonly like a window being banged shut.

1914–16: THIRD SYMPHONY (THE SONG OF THE NIGHT)

One way of describing this masterpiece would be as a kind of halfway house between Wagner and Messiaen. It is a very Wagnerian work, though not in the conventional sense: a setting for solo tenor, chorus and orchestra of a magnificent poem by the thirteenth-century Persian mystic poet Jalal'ad-Din Rumi which evokes the 'transcendental beauty' of an eastern night.

> Oh, do not sleep, friend, through this night.
> You a soul, while we are suff'ring through this night.
> Banish slumber from your eyes!
> The great secret is revealed in this night.
> You are Jove in the high heavens,
> Round heav'n's starry dome you circle in this night!
> Like an eagle fly above!
> Now a hero is your soul in this night.
> Such a quiet, others sleep . . .
> I and God alone together in this night!
> What a roar! Joy arises,
> Truth with gleaming wing is shining in this night!
> Do not sleep, friend,
> If I slumbered until sunrise,
> I should never, never see this night again!
> Thoroughfares on earth are silent,
> There behold the starry roads of this night.
> Leo, Orion,
> Sagittarius and the Virgin blood-red gleam through this night.
> Saturn binds with fateful powers,
> Venus floats in golden rain through this night.
> Silence binds my tongue with fetters,
> But I speak though tongueless in this night![1]

[1] Translated by Ann and Adam Czerniawscy.

Szymanowski sets the text as a single slow movement bisected (between the lines 'Now a hero is your soul in this night' and 'Such a quiet, others sleep . . .') by a scherzo-like intermezzo for orchestra alone – an oriental dance which now attains a boisterousness verging on the martial (trumpet and horn alarms), now pauses as if to listen in rapt attention to the music of the spheres (wordless chorus). The final section brings a glassy-sounding, an almost surrealistic reminiscence of the dance-motif (Ex. 7) on celesta at the soloist's 'Thoroughfares on earth are silent':

Ex.7   Symphony No.3 *(Song of the Night)*

It is as if Szymanowski thought of this scherzo-intermezzo as evoking the 'clamour and tumult' of earthly activity, an episode which impinges only momentarily on the divine consciousness and then disappears altogether. As Rumi says in another poem: 'On every side is clamour and tumult, in every street are torches and candles / For tonight the teeming world gives birth to the world everlasting.'

Although Szymanowski is concerned primarily to distil the essence of the poetic thought, he contrives in the final section some memorable touches of word-painting – the inspired simplicity of 'Such a quiet, others sleep . . .' with its open-fifth chords (piano and harps *soli*) and fermatas; the buzzing organ-pedal and closed-mouth howl of the chorus at 'What a roar! Joy arises', culminating in a chromatic starburst of woodwinds and *glissando* strings; the descending chromatic piano triads to depict the 'starry roads'; the harp glissandos of Venus's 'golden rain'; the impassioned ardour with which the music takes wing and soars aloft at 'Like an eagle fly above! / Now a hero is your soul in this night'; the Wagnerian appoggiaturas of yearning at 'If I slumbered until sunrise / I should never, never see this night again!'

Jalal'ad-Din Rumi (1207–1273), widely regarded as one of the greatest of all mystic poets writing in Persian, was the spiritual leader of the *Mevleviya* order of dervishes whose ritual whirling dance caused them to be known as the Whirling Dervishes. His work embraced all the tenets of classical Sufism, a form of Islamic mysticism whose poetic expression concentrates much on the matter of a personal love-relationship between man and God. A wandering dervish, Shamsoddin Tabriz, appeared to Rumi as the manifestation of the Eternal Beloved, as the 'chosen mouthpiece of the Deity'. Eventually Shams disappeared, possibly killed by jealous disciples; and in his search for the Beloved Rumi became a lyric poet of the first order. Among his later works is the *Diwan-i Shams-i Tabriz*, a collection of lyrical poems or 'ghazels' all inspired by his love and yearning for Shams, and it was from this work that Szymanowski derived the text for his Symphony. Most probably he was not unaware that Rumi's experiences of mystical love seem all to have been with men; but 'mystical' is the operative word: the Ideal Man is regarded as the mirror of God's attributes, so that union with the Beloved is one-and-the-same as union with the Divine. Nor can this union be represented other than through symbols of sensual as well as spiritual intoxication: perception of the soul is through the senses, the senses through the soul:

Joyful the moment when we sat in the bower, Thou and I;
In two forms and with two faces – with one soul, Thou and I.
The colour of the garden and the song of the birds give the elixir of
    immortality
The instant we come into the orchard, Thou and I.

We may interpret *The Song of the Night* – Szymanowski's music no less than Rumi's poem – both as an ardent love-song and as a hymn to the wonder of night. Ultimately the two are synonymous, since for Rumi, as for all great mystics, the phenomena of the natural world are all signs and symbols which both veil and reveal the transcendent presence of God. As he says in one of his aphorisms, 'The hidden world has its clouds and rain, but of a different kind. Its sky and sunshine are of a different kind. This is made apparent only to the refined ones – those not deceived by the seeming completeness of the ordinary world.' In this way a poem such as *The Song of the Night* speaks, or rather whispers, the secret language of the visible universe: the night is image and sacrament of eternal joys and wonders and delights, just as the apples and wine and love-making of the *Song of Solomon* refer to divine and unfathomable mysteries. The link with Wagner comes surely through Novalis, who wrote:

Aside I turn to the holy, ineffable, mysterious night . . . praise be unto the world's queen, the high herald of sacred worlds, the fostering-nurse of blessed love! She sends thee to me, tender Beloved, lovely sun of the Night. I wake now, for I am thine and mine: thou hast proclaimed to me the Night as life and made me human. Consume my body with spirit-fire that I may ethereally commingle more intensely with thee, and that the bridal night may last then for ever!

Here, in one of the undoubted sources of Wagner's *Tristan* poem, is expressed through overtly sexual imagery a romantic conception of night as representing the principle of intuitive knowledge, spiritual truth beyond the reality of objects. Tristan and Isolde find day a delusion and fulfilment only in the night; that the influence of Chopin's chromatic harmony (Chopin who was the first to raise the instrumental nocturne to a high level of expressive eloquence) is particularly marked in Act II of *Tristan* is surely significant in respect of Szymanowski's genealogy, for this act is the first large-scale orchestral 'Song of the Night' in music. At this moment Wagner's link with Impressionism is forged, for his style begins to change from the relatively explicit to the allusive and the evocative; and night, *harmonie du soir*, is the catalyst. Here is the fountainhead of the Third Symphony in the matter of its poetic burden. Yet for its expression in orchestral terms we have to move forward to *Parsifal*, in which, as Robert W. Gutman has well said,[1]

a tenuous, fluctuating Impressionistic light replaces the glow of *Tristan* . . . the music hovers and evaporates like kaleidoscopic images of Symbolist poetry. The atmosphere of the whole work is dream-like, the musical texture transparent, rare and vaporous. . . . The world of musical Impressionism arose from the opera's wondrous orchestral textures. . . .

One could easily describe *The Song of the Night* in these terms, and when Wagner told Cosima that he wanted the colour of *Parsifal* to have 'the softness and shimmer of silk', to be like 'cloud layers that keep separating and combining again', he was also voicing the ideals of many an impressionist tone-poet who came in his wake. Debussy marvellously described the orchestral colour of *Parsifal* as 'éclairée par derrière' – illuminated from behind.

A closer antecedent of *The Song of the Night* is Skryabin's *Prometheus*, from which the symphony may well derive its mystical aura, its sustained expression of ecstasy, its one-movement symphonic design, its (partly) wordless chorus, its huge orchestra, its climactic organ, its use of the piano (not, admittedly, as a *concertante* instrument but nevertheless as a supremely important textural element – as indeed it is in the First Violin Concerto and in *King*

[1] *Richard Wagner – the Man, his Mind and his Music.*

Roger). For all its moments of a truly cosmic grandeur this is in no way a 'choral symphony' in the Beethovenian or Mahlerian sense; 'symphony–cantata' would be an apter designation, but too cumbrous for what is essentially a poetic mood-picture on an epic scale. The choral contribution consists as much in its actual sound and colour as in its enunciating of the words; as in Delius, the voices are an end in themselves rather than a means to an end. Although the composer sanctioned performance of the work without chorus, this involves a disfiguring cut and removes an entire expressive dimension. A tradition also has grown up whereby the tenor soloist is replaced by a soprano; but in view of the fact that the other 'soloist' is a solo violin – the 'soprano' of the string family – a natural spectrum of colour is obtained only if Szymanowski's original intentions are respected. There is, too, at least one sound (in more than one sense) practical reason for so doing: namely a phrase which Szymanowski directs the solo tenor to sing in unison with the chorus tenors ('You a soul, while we are suff'ring through this night'). If the soprano sings it we hear it of course an octave too high and the composer's intention is falsified.

In regard both to thematic matter and formal manner the influence of oriental music points the symphony forward in the direction of Messiaen. No attempt is made to approximate to sonata structure; an overall ABA design is 'symphonically' unified by quite other means, and Szymanowski's craftsmanship is, as always, impeccable, however unorthodox the end product. Let us note, for instance, the extraordinarily felicitous skill of the transition which leads from the central dance-episode back to the immobility of the mystic midnight hour. Here a tiny segment of the dance-theme (Ex. 7) is repeated over and over again, ever slower and softer, while beneath it a derivative of Ex. 8 – which belongs to the outer panels of the triptych – begins to sound as re-echoing and overlapping horn-calls:

Ex.8 Symphony No.3 *(Song of the Night)*

Of course, the fabric is strengthened by motivic links between sections in the usual way: an important theme belonging to the dance-panel is found embedded at an early stage in the first section and is recalled in the last on solo violin and clarinet only a few bars before the end, while we have already noted the spectral celesta reminiscence of Ex. 7 during the tenor's last solo. But the general *procedure*, the way the music is literally 'composed', is different from the type of continuously evolving argument that we are accustomed to find in a symphony. Instead there are short sections repeated, varied, transposed, realigned and rejuxtaposed in a totally non-developing, non-Western way.

Also non-Western is Szymanowski's use of short motifs of restricted intervallic range (as in Exx. 7 and 8), which thus lend themselves readily to repetition and elaboration and produce the kind of incantatory, mesmeric effect we associate with oriental music. The result is a kind of motion-in-stasis very characteristic of true oriental music and so of Messiaen. For instance, the basic musical substance of bars 14–23 is identical with that of bars 1–13, but all kinds of subtle changes have been wrought in the texture; the second half of the dance is an (apparently literal) repetition of the first, yet a second hearing reveals an infinite variety of textural modifications. The great apotheosis of the finale has already been foreshadowed in all its essential aspects by the impassioned climax of the first section; but it is quite misleading to make use of terms like 'exposition' or 'recapitulation' in this context since the manner of thinking is fundamentally alien to those Western concepts of 'moments in time'. Rather do we have to do here with the 'continuous continuation' of the Orient in which ideas do not so much progress horizontally as expand vertically. The general slowness of the harmonic pulse, even in the dance-episodes which appear to be fast-moving, is another contributory factor to the feeling of stasis (one of the lessons Western musicians have learned from the East is that movement need not in itself be dynamic). Striking too are those passages in which the measured metric units of Western music come to exist on paper only, not in sound. The solo violin and flute music between figs. 81 and 82, for instance, leaves us unaware of beats and bar-lines: the impression is one of improvisation, this freedom-with-the bar being less a matter of sympathetic performance than an inbuilt conceptual feature. Texture and ornamentation become structural components, and many moments in *The Song of the Night* consist in nothing but texture, sonority, exquisitely imagined sound *per se*.

No pedantic description of these delicious aural *frissons* and *parfums* is necessary, for the listener need only perceive them sensually for himself; but it is perhaps worth while drawing attention to the pre-Bartókian night-music on alternating clarinets, to the cello glissandi which Szymanowski probably found in *Daphnis et Chloë* but which bring to English ears an interesting pre-echo of Britten's 'forest murmurs' in *A Midsummer Night's Dream*; and the hypnotically repeated ostinati for piano, celesta, harps and glockenspiel at the two major climaxes already mentioned foreshadow the gamelan-derived sonorities of *Turangalîla*. Moreover, it has been remarked of oriental music (and of Messiaen's work) that its peculiar structure (determined of course by its psychological and philosophical motivation) negates traditional concepts of beginning, progress and end; for the oriental picture of time is essentially cyclic, eternally repetitive. Likewise, *The Song of the Night* seems neither properly to begin or end: a low long-held pedal C is distinguishable at its coming in, at its two major climaxes, and at its going out to the wonderful night-wind-like whispering or murmuring of viola and cello glissandi in natural harmonics. In other words, one's aural impression is that this long low C is actually going on all the time, always has been and always will be, not merely when we happen to be hearing it made musically incarnate in the form of Szymanowski's *Song of the Night*.

The Third Symphony was composed between 1914 and 1916, but a projected performance in St Petersburg under Alexander Siloti later in 1916 failed to materialise owing to the political turmoil. At the time of the world première, given in London in November 1921 by Albert Coates, the composer was absent in America. Just as well, one imagines, for the chorus was replaced by an organ (horrific shades of the 'alternative' *Daphnis et Chloë*) and the tenor, incredibly, by a solo cello. Not until February 1928 was a complete performance mounted in Lwow.

1916: FIRST VIOLIN CONCERTO

The First Violin Concerto is probably Szymanowski's most approachable score. It was written in the summer and autumn of 1916 and, like the *Mythes*, was the fruit of his collaboration with

Kochański. What in effect evolved from this collaboration was a new concept of the violin as a *concertante* instrument. Of Delius's Violin Concerto, also composed in 1916, a distinguished exponent (probably Jean Pougnet) remarked to Beecham: 'It's not a concerto but a most lovely poem.' Szymanowski's is both lovely poem *and* concerto; as in the *Mythes* the virtuoso element, though vitally present, is sublimated in the interests of the type of poetic, private quality of expression which we can trace back through Sibelius to Mendelssohn; this line of development is essentially different from the bigger, bolder, full-heartedly symphonic cast of the Brahms, Tchaikovsky (and Elgar) concertos in which the public/private dichotomy of sonata form is perpetuated.

The latter is not at all suited to the expression of faery and fantasy, and there is absolutely nothing 'of-the-earth, earthy' about Szymanowski's concerto, as the very first bars make a point of telling us. This opening has never failed to provoke admiring comment. Its fantastic little dashes and flashes of sound, bitonally propelled, fluttering and dancing like a thousand tiny fires, suggest endless parallels, musical and otherwise: a distant firework display; a *pointilliste* canvas; an imperial Fabergé jewel aglitter with sequins; César Franck's wonderful definition of the nervous appeal of Debussy's music as 'de la musique sur la pointe des aiguilles', music on needle-points. Skryabin is an obvious influence here. Another composer who springs to mind is Mendelssohn, but a Mendelssohn raised to the nth power. In fact the Concerto is quite literally a 'midsummer night's dream', for its literary inspiration was *May Night*, a poem by Miciński which intermingles mythological and pantheistic elements:

> Asses in crowns settle majestically on the grass –
> fireflies are kissing the wild rose –
> and Death shimmers on the pond
> and plays a frivolous song.
>   Ephemerids
>   fly into dance –
> oh, flowers of the lakes, Nereids!
> Pan plays his pipes in the oak grove.
>   Ephemerids
>   fly into dance,
>   fly into dance –
>   plaited in amorous embrace
>   eternally young and holy –
>   stabbed with a lethal dart.

In the twinkling blue water
golden crucians and roach,
and patient kingfishers
gaze with their eyes of steel –
and on the trees the hammering of the little blacksmiths,
amid the sorb, red crooked-beaks
and kestrels with eyes like tinder –
merrily whistling and chanting
I fly: here over the water – there under the trees . . . .
In the woods are glades as if appointed
for these nocturnal revels.
All the birds pay tribute to me,
for today I wed a Goddess . . .
And now we stand by the lake,
in crimson blossoms,
in flowing tears of joy, with rapture and fear,
burning in amorous conflagrations:
the fire seizes these aged trees
and they shed tears of pitch,
and the familiar gull from the Polar seas
describes a halo over us. . . .[1]

Inasmuch as birds of various species are a prominent feature of this fantastic dreamscape, it is not surprising to find here, as in the nocturnal Third Symphony, some fascinating pre-echoes of the night world of Bartók and of Messiaen. The *fons et origo* of all such music, as of much else in musical Impressionism, is the *Waldweben* episode in Wagner's *Siegfried*: here, for the first time, birdsong (however heavily stylised) enters Western music as a symbol of mystic innocence, a voice of man's craving for a heaven beyond consciousness. The preludial twitterings, flickerings and darting motions of Szymanowski's concerto are no more than highly evolved, highly elaborated variations on the same theme.

If the concerto really is Mendelssohn or Wagner 'raised to the nth power', we may legitimately ask: raised by whom or by what? – since the state of mind it expresses is one conceivable to most of us in terms only of dream or intoxication. Was it, in fact, drug-inspired? After the first performance in Warsaw the composer told Kochański that all his expectations had been surpassed: 'The sound is so magical that people here were completely transfixed. And just imagine, Paweł-eczka, *the violin is continually on top*. . . .' The solo voice floats way above in consistently disembodied ecstasy, the artificially induced ecstasy of a 'trip'; the score glows and shimmers in an unearthly light.

[1] Translated by Sylvia and Benjamin Shoshan.

As a translation into music of the poem's divine midsummer madness it is fabulously successful: never are we allowed to forget that the progenitor and protagonist is Pan/Dionysus, and though exaltation is the keynote, from time to time darker, more sinister elements try to break the surface. A particular instance is the passage bridging the cadenza to the main climax with its madly fleeing semiquavers, its menacing trombone solo and tremolo strings shrinking in apprehension. One of the major themes, in 6/8, is bacchanalian in character and seems to exhort both solo violin and orchestra to outbursts of some savagery (e.g., the low trumpets' exhausted climax which introduces the cadenza). Other invitations to the dance are less obtrusively delivered – a slow three-in-the-bar with soft tambourine shakes suggesting some ancient hieratic dance (*Lento*, four bars after figure 43), a graceful but short-lived mazurka (fig. 63), both performed in air heavy-laden with incense.

The Concerto's formal scheme is one of Szymanowski's great triumphs. In this case 'form' is not so much formula as spontaneous formulation. Music exists in time; time in this 'form' is here, but has lost its self-consciousness, its divisive quality. We can no longer neatly pigeon-hole the phases through which the music passes, for it is concerned predominantly, not with measures and locations, but with being and meaning. Yet the 'spontaneity' is an illusion; here an inexorable logic hides itself. Link is added silently, but faultlessly, to link; the argument carries us with it from point to point towards a determined goal, but unawares. Take the work to pieces, as Jim Samson has done, and one finds it is constructed with a mathematical precision; every piece can be taken out and replaced in order. Here is Samson's tabulated analysis:

1 Fantasy 1
  First quick section – Climax 1
  Fantasy 2

2 Thematic Group A
  Fantasy 3
  Development of A – Climax 2

3 Second quick section – Thematic Group B
  Fantasy 4
  Development of A – Climax 3

4 Thematic Group C – Climax 4
   Development of B
   Cadenza

5 Climax 5 based on A
   Fantasy 5
   Closing reference to C

This is, of course, merely a diagram of the music's skeleton and can give no indication whatever of its incomparable seamless unity, the total absence of artificial 'joins', the way in which it seems (to quote Debussy on Mussorgsky's form) to be made up of 'successive minute touches mysteriously linked together by means of an instinctive clairvoyance'. Here, however, 'clairvoyance' involves consummate technical expertise: the expertise which, for instance, seems to draw the solo instrument out of the bosom of the orchestra through the simple expedient of causing it to sound the same note as is sounding, or has just ceased to sound, in the orchestra; the illusion created is that the solo violin has been playing all the time, materialising and dematerialising at will. Rapid tempo contrasts are avoided, and Adam Walaciński sees in the patterned fluidity of the entire formal concept a distinct effort to free music from the mechanical rigidities of metre and bar-line. Not that links with traditional forms are totally dissolved. At times (to use an obnoxious but useful piece of contemporary jargon) we may think to find ourselves in a scherzo-ish or slow-movement or recapitulation-like 'situation'; but none of them goes quite according to (our) plan, as indeed in dreams things tend not to. At no point, however, is there any musical or emotional break; the only self-consciously dramatic 'event' is the cadenza, and this is strategically placed so as to launch with a quasi-Straussian orchestral opulence the biggest, best and most unashamedly erotic climax of all (the sexual connotations of the poems do not need much detecting). After consummating his 'wedding with the goddess' the dreamer awakes to find himself on the cold hillside (ethereal harmonics and *pizzicato*).

Inasmuch as the concerto is one long never-ceasing 'song', there are no set 'arias' or long-lined themes as such, rather a series of motifs which give direction to the rhapsodic progress of the work. Ex. 9 is the clinching theme which dominates the main climax just described. Its magic is contained not only in the sweep and surge of its line but in its underlying harmonic progression. A valued asset of the family of 'dominant' chords has always been their way of sounding both logical and unexpected, and the resolution of the tonic chord of E in bar 1 of Ex. 9 into a dominant thirteenth on A flat in bar 2 is one of those harmonic surprises almost physically sensual in its impact:

Ex.9 Violin Concerto No.1

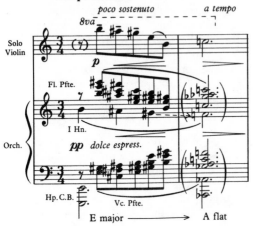

This kind of frankly romantic passion inflames the concerto no less than 'La Fontaine d'Aréthuse', and has certainly always helped to smooth the passage of both works with their audiences.

That the Concerto was specifically conceived with the 'captivating sweetness' of Kochański's tone in mind can scarcely be doubted. In his classic treatise on orchestration Cecil Forsyth refers to the 'masculine' character of the solo violin and its 'feminine' counterpart, the solo cello. In this case, however, the roles are surely reversed: the soloist sings with all the irresistible, inebriating femininity of the Dionysus-figure in *King Roger*. The Concerto is an apotheosis of instrumental 'song'. When Szymanowski once described Poland's true national music as 'not the stiffened ghost of the polonaise or mazurka, nor a fugue on the *Chmielu* wedding song . . . rather the solitary, joyful, carefree song of the nightingale in a fragrant May night in Poland', he surely had in mind his own First Violin Concerto, a unique masterpiece not merely of Polish impressionist romanticism but of all music.

1917: THIRD PIANO SONATA

At the height of his Impressionist period Szymanowski began to offset his many programmatic preoccupations by reverting to 'pure' music, diverting classical forms to his own purposes. The *Etudes* (1916) as well as the Third Piano Sonata belong in this category, though as we might expect both show the influence of the period of stylistic reorientation which had intervened since the composer's earlier efforts in those particular genres (Debussy's later 'abstract' work is a parallel case). Harmonically, structurally and texturally the Sonata bears broad traces of Impressionism, although the music is not intended to 'evoke' anything in particular.

The piece is in one continuous movement but clearly embraces the four conventional phases of the orthodox sonata. These phases are linked not only by a characteristically individual process of thematic cross-indexing but also by the simple expedient of making the first note of each new movement identical with the *last* note of the one before. Szymanowski reverses the usual order of thematic precedence in a sonata first movement: the second subject, rather than the first, is the principal *dramatis persona*. On its first appearance the latter has an air of pathos, but subsequently proves sturdy enough to support the mighty clamour of bell-ringing which forms the climax of the development and which is one of the finest passages in the Sonata (see over).

The first movement's *first* subject is reactivated in the central section of the song-like, elegiac slow movement, which also engages various flickering figures destined to play an important part in the scherzo. The latter is so brief as to be construed more as a preamble to the fugal finale than as a movement in its right. Here, and in the fugue, Szymanowski approaches to the motoric, percussive style of Bartók as displayed in such works as the Piano Sonata (written in 1926, nine years after Szymanowski's Third) and in the Second Piano Concerto. The shape of the fugue subject is no stranger to us, having been adumbrated at some point in each of the preceding movements. Of all Szymanowski's virtuoso fugal displays this is perhaps the most dazzling; inasmuch as the writing is totally a product of his mature style, he repays his debt to Reger with generous interest. The triumphant climax of the movement, and of the Sonata, is the return of the first movement's second theme in logical and satisfying conjunction with every conceivable permutation and derivation of the fugue subject.

Ex.10   Sonata No.3

Andante *(ma con passione)*

1917: FIRST STRING QUARTET

The two string quartets make up the sum-total of Szymanowski's contribution to the chamber music repertoire: a pity, in view of the professional skill and understanding with which he writes for piano and stringed instruments. The First Quartet is a transitional piece which in its new linear and formal clarity and contrapuntal consistency flows back in the classical mainstream (or is it forward to neo-classicism?) and clears the decks for Szymanowski's forthcoming discovery and assimilation of folksong. That the composer should have been drawn to this medium at this time is in itself significant, for with four solo strings the possibilities for elaborate impressionistic effects of colour or atmosphere are limited.

The new simplicity is epitomised in the opening and closing bars of the first movement: the opening consists of a motif of common chords (C major, D major, E major), while the end is an ordinary plagal cadence – though there is nothing common or ordinary about the way Szymanowski uses them. The sonata form in which the movement is cast is, however, for the mature Szymanowski, untypically regular, and the expressive chromaticism of the second subject is reminiscent of the composer's earlier manner. The bipartite slow movement – one of Szymanowski's most beautiful – asserts the supremacy of melody in its very subtitle ('in moda d'una canzona') and reintroduces the chordal motif from the opening of the first movement; the rapt, poetic quality of the second part is a kind of after-ring of the Impressionist sound-world from which this very 'abstract' work is in the process of moving away.

The last movement is a scherzo which also does duty as a finale, since a projected fourth movement was never written. It is a fugal sonata-allegro in which each instrument is written in a different key, but which sounds considerably less discordant than it looks on paper. The first subject (Ex. 11) bears some resemblance to the fugue in Milhaud's *Protée*, one of the earliest polytonal *tours-de-force*.

Ex.11   String Quartet No.1
Scherzando alla burlesca
Vivace ma non troppo

We have no evidence that Szymanowski knew much of Milhaud at this time; it is safer to assume that the strong bitonal inclinations already present in the Polish composer's own work led him naturally to expand on them, particularly in the context of a scherzo in which 'wrong' notes are permitted to sound funny. Szymanowski gives the form a droll twist at the end: the second subject begins to surface again but quickly tires of the effort and wraps up the proceedings with an 'ordinary' C major perfect cadence, *pizzicato*.

1918: SONGS OF AN INFATUATED MUEZZIN

Only in this work do Szymanowski's oriental stylisations teeter on the borderline between piquancy and vulgarity; his innate taste, and the fact that he was before all things an artist in sound, save him – but only just. Iwaszkiewicz's poems describe a muezzin's[1] infatuation with a young girl, yet the emotion is no more 'real' than in the *Songs of a Fairy Princess*; the stylisations serve as a distancing agent, just like the child-princess's world of make-believe in the earlier cycle. This is why, although the muezzin equates love of the beautiful girl with love of Allah, the link with the Third Symphony is literally skin-deep: just as the muezzin's concerns are frankly carnal, so the musical substance is decorative, exotically pictorial. We must turn to the Third Symphony and *King Roger* for profound and meaningful contemplation of East–West relations. Meantime, in the interest of pure sensuous delight much can detain us here: the dreamy dawnscape of no. 3; in no. 4 the languid evocation of the city gleaming in the midday heat but suddenly coming to life in excited dance (marked *agitatissimo*) as the beloved goes to her bath; a serenade to lull her 'golden dreams', heavily spiced with chromatic harmony and a drowsy, quasi-Delian barcarolle-like lilt. The orchestral transcriptions add a new dimension of colour, but it was as well that Szymanowski began to turn to other sources of inspiration before the fibre of his orientalism had the opportunity to coarsen.

1918–24: KING ROGER

The theme of *King Roger* is the oft-developed one of Apollo, the embodiment of order and self-discipline, versus Dionysus, the god

---

[1] The Mohammedan crier who proclaims the hours of prayer from a minaret; hence the recurrent and extended melismas in both the voice and piano part.

of sensual freedom and self-indulgence. A mere seven years before Szymanowski conceived *King Roger*, Thomas Mann's novella *Death in Venice* had been similarly motivated; the two works also have in common the theme of homosexual attraction, even though in *King Roger* it is much less explicit than in *Death in Venice*. Here too Walter Pater enters the scene, for Szymanowski was an admirer of the latter's short stories *Apollo in Picardy* and *Denys l'Auxerrois* to the extent of considering them as possibilities for music-dramatic treatment. In both the pagan deity of Dionysus, blond and beautiful, reappears in human form in medieval times; for a brief spell his influence is intoxicating and inspiring, but the upshot is madness, violence and death.

Szymanowski was clearly fascinated by the ambiguous nature of such a figure, by the perilously insubstantial dividing line between the higher and lower parts of man's nature, between the god and the beast. *Les extrêmes se touchent*; excesses of whatever kind are ultimately destructive. But if in both *Death in Venice* and *Denys l'Auxerrois* the unbridled sway of Dionysus leads to emotional and physical breakdown, *King Roger* purports to effect a reconciliation. In this respect the opera's resolution, for which Szymanowski re-fashioned the text himself, differs significantly from the original libretto provided by Jarosław Iwaszkiewicz. The latter closed with Roger's surrender to the Stranger God; in Szymanowski's version he rejects him, not in any hysteria of self-abnegation, but rather in the spirit of Tippett's 'I would know my shadow and my light: then shall I at last be whole.' Roger is from the outset irresistibly attracted to the mysterious Shepherd, but at the instance of the Church starts by opposing him and even attempting to fetter him. Later he yields to him, only to discover that the religion of pleasure which he represents is in its own way just as much of a stereotype as the ritual dogmatism of the Church; hence he rejects both, makes a symbolic sacrifice and greets the new day with an exultant hymn.

Not for nothing, surely, can this theme of the fundamental rift in the human psyche – the conflict between man (Apollo) and beast (Dionysus in his most destructive guise) – be seen to be a major preoccupation of artists at a time when the onset of 'decadent' themes (which naturally led to the evolving of 'decadent' techniques for their expression) culminated irreparably in the rending of European civilisation during the 1914–18 war. Significantly the pervasively disruptive chromaticism of Roger's music settles conclusively on C major in his final apotheosis to the sun. Szymanowski himself had for some time been seeking the rock-firm diatonic stability of Polish peasant music as the basis for new stylistic directions. For him, clearly, *King Roger* was purgation and renewal, and as such one of the key works in his output.

The departure-point of *King Roger* was Euripides' *Bacchae*, whose puritanical King Pentheus represses Dionysian urges in himself and persecutes what he is secretly attracted to. Roger is altogether a worthier adversary of the god who, in his more positive guise, inspires all imaginative artistic enterprise, all that urges the common-place into the rare. The real Roger was ruler of Sicily, the meeting-place of classical, Moorish and Norman cultures. He was at one and the same time patron of the sciences, lover of the arts, aesthete, intellectual, diplomatist, idealist and despot, and presided over a court at Palermo which was easily the most brilliant of twelfth-century Europe, giving as it did a home to many of the best scientific and artistic talents of the European and Arab worlds. Herein undoubtedly lay one of the strongest reasons for the appeal of *King Roger* to Szymanowski. When in 1918 Iwaszkiewicz sent the composer a draft of his libretto, Szymanowski wrote in reply:

Byzantine–Arabic palace interiors would be most desirable. Imagine the muted gold and the rigidity of the mosaic figures in the background, of let us say Arabic filigree, dancing . . . what delightful barbaric wealth . . . deep contrasts of oddly welded worlds, search for the hidden meaning. . . .

The hand, or rather the acute imaginative eye, of Szymanowski can surely be seen behind the scrupulously detailed instructions for the scenic design of each of the opera's three acts.

A description of such ornately opulent complexity scarcely envisages any rapid process of scene-change, and in itself provides a clue as to the real nature of the work. It is, in fact, scarcely more 'operatic' or conventionally dramatic than Bartók's *Bluebeard's Castle* (one of a number of contemporary or near-contemporary works with which *King Roger* shows coincidental affinities, others being Stravinsky's *Nightingale* and, as earlier mentioned, the operatic work of Schreker).

As Zofia Helman points out in her preface to the full score in the Collected Edition, *King Roger* is not so much 'pure' opera as a hybrid stage-spectacle embracing elements also of Wagnerian music-drama, oratorio and mystery play. Wagner would have approved the setting of the text as more or less continuous recitative unbroken (save in a few significant instances) by formal arias; the use of leitmotifs; and the preponderance of the orchestra. On the other hand, the fact that little actual drama takes place on stage tends to translate *King Roger* to the sphere of oratorio, as does the integral part of the chorus in each act ('tableau' would be a better word inasmuch as there is so little outward action). In fact *King Roger* could be quite satisfactorily performed in concert; the eye would be far more conscious of the absence of scenery and sets – which marvellously complement the character of the music – than of the protagonists' inability to move about. The visual importance of the scenic backdrop – which changes for each act but remains unchanged *within* each – is what calls to mind the medieval mystery play, together with the ritual element which likewise is a star feature.

The setting of the first act is Byzantine; the curtain rises to disclose the interior of Palermo Cathedral.

At the back in the centre [prescribes Szymanowski] is the gigantic hemispherical vaulting of the apse above the high altar, separated from the nave by a row of pillars in many-coloured marbles . . . the many arches and vaultings are supported on huge temples. The inside of the vault of the apse is filled by an enormous mosaic icon of Christ with a thin, ascetic face and black sunken eyes . . . the general impression is one of dim gold, richly glowing in the light of the thousands of candles which are burning in chandeliers hung from the ceiling.

A solemn mass is in progress, and Szymanowski follows in the wake of Meyerbeer and Wagner in exploiting the spectacular magnificence of church ceremonies, boys' voices as in the first act of *Parsifal* included. But whereas Meyerbeer's ecclesiastical scenes served a purely exterior, pomp-and-circumstantial purpose, Szymanowski, like Wagner in *Parsifal*, makes theatrical capital out of ethical and religious attitudes in themselves. The setting is very much to the dramatic point, and Szymanowski's Byzantine stylisations – which include the medieval techniques of organum and fauxbourdon – not only evoke the hieratic, formal splendour of Eastern ritual worship but also create a sense of austerity and doctrinal rigidity. That he numbers among his archaisms a Protestant chorale as well as Byzantine hymns and incantations should surprise no one who recalls the chapel in Palermo where friendly Norman arches, reminiscent of many English country churches, suddenly join company with a Byzantine mosaic and an Arab west wall, the result miraculously bearing no trace of stylistic incongruity. Much the same could be said of *King Roger*, an immediate and all-important clue to its musical homogeneity being the fact that the germ of the Shepherd's aria (Ex. 12b) – the theme associated with 'his' God – is none other than the Byzantine chant with which the opera begins (Ex. 12a). Again *les extrêmes se touchent*, yet conflict with each other throughout the first act.

Ex.12   *King Roger*

(a)   **Lento assai**

(b)   **Andante tranquillissimo e dolce**

The recurrent Byzantine music comes both to express and symbolise the Establishment's overt hostility to the Shepherd and his teaching, most powerfully in the climactic ensemble in which the voices of reason – those of the sage Edrisi and of Roger's Queen, Roxana – soar in impassioned entreaty over the Church's granite-like triads insistently repeating the same phrase over a *basso ostinato* with dogmatic inflexibility: the Shepherd must be condemned. This is one of the finest moments in the opera, and a turning point: Roger has no time for superstitious hysteria, and in any case is already predisposed to tolerance for the Shepherd from motives still but dimly defined in his mind. Heedless of the Church which continues balefully to mutter, he enjoins the Shepherd first to go in peace, then voluntarily to return that night to give a true account of himself.

The Shepherd's 'otherness' is movingly revealed in the orchestral passage which accompanies the moment of his first appearance, music in whose ethereal beauty and tranquillity we immediately feel the air of distant planets. It haunts the memory, expresses the inexpressible and is quintessential Szymanowski. Its ambience, if not its specific substance, is invoked again in Act II when the Shepherd tells of the distant parts whence he has come: white Benares, the lotus land of Indra, the waters of the Ganges. His most important theme, however, is strategically held in reserve by Szymanowski to appear only as the issue of the act's main climax already described: an enigmatic motif of chromatic caste which stands for the Shepherd's power over the king. For Roger this is the moment of truth, and explains why he abruptly changes his mind and orders the Shepherd to reappear that night. Of Roger's own *Leitmotif* comparatively little is heard; it makes a telling first appearance in the opening scene where its lugubrious minor thirds, intruding into and simultaneously lifting the audience beyond the stylised splendour of the church music, immediately signifies a man not at peace with himself, an Amfortas seeking to heal him of his grievous wound. Like Amfortas too, Roger finds redemption through a young man fair of face – although the latter is anything but a *reiner Narr*, and the way he points to Roger leads in the first instance to destruction rather than salvation.

That the king realises he has unleashed dark forces within himself is made audible within the first few bars of Act II, which takes place in the royal palace and, symbolically, at night. Here the music is not only *im*pressionistic in that it evokes the oppressive languor of the eastern night, but *ex*pressionistic in that it probes deep into the troubled mind of the king, who is in an advanced state of nervous tension. Edrisi enjoins him to listen to the unseen Roxana's wordless quasi-oriental melismata, which resolve into the aria in which she entreats the balsam of the night to cool her consort's pounding heart and incline him to show mercy to the Shepherd. With its thrummed hypnotic throbbing of harps, tenuous, aromatic orchestration and wordless choral music rising and falling in the dusk (like voices of nature, of the night, as in the Third Symphony), this famous set-piece is the sheerest seduction, glamour, enchantment.

Ex.13 *King Roger*

The parallel with Arthur Machen's *Hill of Dreams*[1] is uncanny:

The shadowy air was full of the perfume of eastern things. The attar of roses must have been sprinkled in the foundation . . . all the faery-work of the chancelled stone hovered and glimmered beneath the sky, dark as the violet, dark as wine. The singing voice swelled to rapture and passion as the song chanted the triumph of the Lover and the Beloved, how their souls were melted together as the juice of the grape is mingled in the vintage, how they found the Gate and the Way . . . and every rose in the dusky air was aflame.
. . .

The Shepherd approaches: Roger's uncontrollable agitation is reflected in a dissonant, writhing counterpoint of arabesque fleshed and thickened from an important chromatic motif in Roxana's aria, which is gradually overpowered by another dissonant (and initially distant) counterpoint: the sounding of the watchmen's clarion calls in two keys simultaneously. Here are unmistakable shades of Act II of *Tristan* – the catalyst of night, the Brangäne-like voice of Roxana off-stage, the *Hörnerschall in der Ferne*, Roger in the grip of the kind of excitability not, after all, so far removed from that of Isolde awaiting her lover; he even has his Kurwenal in the form of Edrisi. The Shepherd, unseen as yet, calls Roger's name; the orchestra enters with sweeping waves of harp and transforms his top A from the third of the old key, F, to the fifth of the new, D: it is almost like the opening of magic casements, a momentary glimpse of the Beatific Vision. The Shepherd asserts his own regality in a passionate, tumultuous orchestral development of his 'power' motif which leads to a blazing affirmation of Ex. 12b.

The king is now openly antagonistic to the Shepherd, and they confront each other in a long tortuous scene; its culmination, and the climax of the act, is the Dionysian dance in which the Shepherd casts his spell over the entire court, an important motivic constituent of which is Roxana's chromatic melisma. This, the longest and most elaborate and most magnificent of Szymanowski's many Oriental dance-stylisations, is both musically and dramatically redolent of *Salome*, whose influence in this particular act of *King Roger* is really no less obvious than in the case of *Hagith*. Yet, viewed in the overall context of the opera, everything falls harmoniously into place; much of this is due to Szymanowski's architectural skill. When we reach the end of Act III we realise how careful he has been to balance the varied elements of each act: each contains as its main climax a

[1] See p. 34.

musically stylised act of ritual (the Church's vehement represent-
ations to Roger in I, the dance in II, the Bacchanalian procession in
III), and each features a 'closed' form, an aria, a flight of sustained
melodic invention. In I the Shepherd's aria frames his entry and exit,
in II Roxana woos the king from afar; but in III it is Roger's turn, and
his hymn to the sun is strategically placed: not until he is made whole
and the shadows of the night dispersed, may he, at the apogee of the
opera, make glad his heart in lyrical fullness.

This last act takes place in the ruins of a Greek theatre, and the
music's prevailing colours are therefore Hellenic. The night is
drawing to its close but it is still dark. Framing the weatherworn
rocks, half-shattered columns, fragments of metopes and friezes and
the debris of statues is the 'immense abyss of the sky' and the 'endless
expanse of the sea', which beats heavily and incessantly against the
shore. This is the desolate scene evoked in the restlessly shifting,
bitonal half-light of the strings and in a ghostly dialogue between
clarinet and muted horn with occasional interjections of muted
trumpets; but the music is also expressive of Roger's travel-weary
dejection and generally demoralised state of mind. When the first
distant sounds of the Bacchic revellers creep on his ear (wordless
chorus) we are struck by their similarity to the chanting of the priests
in Act I. The point is crucially reinforced at the climax of the act
when the Shepherd, having revealed himself to Roger in his true
guise of Dionysus, leads all his followers into his realm, not in a wild
dance (as in Act II) but in a ritualised, formalised processional
movement strikingly similar in musical physiognomy to the parallel
passage in Act I – the same major-second *basso ostinato*, ostinati in
other parts, a ponderous, inexorable surge. The motivation of
thraldom is the same, but the expression in this, the opera's true
turning-point and most decisive climax, is incomparably more
ecstatic and reminiscent, in its rhythmic and textural complexity, of
that of *The Song of the Night*. Overlaying everything is the mad
Bacchic piping of the woodwinds which create their own wild,
swarming, riotous counterpoint of arabesque; from a performance
point of view it is almost impossible to prevent their being swamped
by the heavy brass, chorus, soloists and a towering edifice of tremolo
strings, and this is a major disappointment of the Aurora recording.
The doubling of each woodwind part *ad infinitum* might solve the
problem, but is scarcely a practical expedient under normal
circumstances.

Gradually the clamour of Pan and his revellers goes out of earshot, and Roger awaits the dawn. This music is among the most beautiful in Szymanowski: it makes no concessions to conventional notions of musical pictorialisation, but is poetic and evocative in a way utterly personal to the composer. He must have seen some fabulous sunrises during his 'voyages of discovery' in Sicily and Africa, and memories of the first light of dawn flooding the waters to the ecstatic encircling motions of seabirds – gold, blue and white – here coalesce in an impressionistic masterstroke.

Jim Samson has commented on the 'inconclusiveness' of the C major triad which 'prematurely' concludes Roger's hymn to the sun. However, there is an interesting precedent here – the coda of Skryabin's *Prometheus* where, 'dans un vertige', the music hurls itself deliriously forward, alights on an F sharp major triad – and then, without a word of warning, *finis operis*. Again the immediate effect is 'premature and inconclusive'. Could we perhaps in these two cases be dealing with a musical symbol of some blinding moment of revelation which renders superfluous all normal processes of preparation and resolution? It is worth recalling that C major is the home key of the Third Symphony, the work which represents a pantheistic merging of ego-dominated passion into nature. It is possible that the seemingly abrupt final cadences of both *Prometheus* and *King Roger* had some arcane significance for the composers, on the nature of which we can do no more than speculate.

1921: SŁOPIEWNIE

In July 1920 Szymanowski published an article, 'Thoughts on Polish Criticism Today', which registers his newly awakened nationalist consciousness in no uncertain terms: 'Now is the time for us to lay our foundations for the future . . . let our music be *national* in its Polish characteristics but not falter in striving to attain *universality*. Let it be national, but not provincial.' In his first (and highly original) attempt to put his theory into practice he turned to a prominent poet of the *Skamander* movement, Julian Tuwim. Tuwim was much influence by Rimbaud and, like him, much interested both in black magic and in the structure of words in themselves. His *Słopiewnie* – from 'słowo' (word) and 'piewnie' (singing, lament or recitation) – are composed in an invented Slavic-derived language in which old roots are run together in new combinations and word-endings modified. Because of this, and because of the poems' heavy reliance on assonance, alliteration and internal rhyme-schemes, the songs cannot properly be sung in any but the original language.

When Szymanowski spoke of his attempt in *Słopiewnie* to 'crystallise elements of tribal heritage' he was referring no doubt to the inevitably, primordially *musical* articulation of emotion (both human and non-human) in such forms as the nightingale's song in no. 1,[1] halloos and shouts of ecstasy in nos. 2 and 4, ancient rites of worship in no. 3, wailing in no. 5. Hence the use of melodic, rhythmic and harmonic formulae derived from folkmusic, particularly the descending 'Sabała' motif of the Tatra mountaineers, a basic melodic shape which is to recur frequently in Szymanowski's work from now on (see Ex. 14 from *Harnasie*, p. 84). It appears at the start of no. 3, 'St Francis', which also introduces archaic organum-like effects (parallel fifths, thirds and triads) of a kind that are later to appear, deprived of their quotation marks, in the *Stabat Mater*. No. 4 shows more folk influence, this time refracted through Stravinsky: open fourths and fifths, short melodic phrases incantatorily repeated in changing geometric patterns, ostinati which either repeat figures or vary them so that the attention is kept fixed or perpetually realerted. The last song, 'Wanda' – the title refers to the legendary Polish princess who, about the year 700, sacrificed herself by drowning in the river Vistula to propitiate the deity through whose intervention she had led her troops to victory – combines in masterly fashion all the new-old elements in music that is both evocative, programmatic and elegiac.

1923–31: HARNASIE

Góral folk music (i.e. that of the Tatras or Polish highlands) can be traced back at least as far as Jan Krzeptowski (known as 'Sabała'), mountain-guide, singer, violinist, story-teller, hunter and, according to legend, highland robber. He gave his name to the motif already noted in *Słopiewnie* (see Ex. 14) and established a folk-musical tradition passed on through families of musicians. The most important of these in the early twentieth century were the Obrochtas,

---

[1] As we have seen, the *Songs of a Fairy Princess* were in a sense all nightingale's songs, all written for the coloratura voice of Stasia Szymanowska – who also happens to be the dedicatee of *Słopiewnie*.

headed by Bartek Obrochta, a good friend of Szymanowski. Obrochta's 'violin trio' (two fiddles and a three-string bass) was greatly admired by the composer for their remarkable improvisations in heterophony.[1] Other features of Góral music are an unorthodox kind of polyphonic singing for high men's and deep women's voices, and the use of pedal-points – either the bagpipe-fifth or the less familiar and considerably more dissonant minor second. The hypersophisticated Szymanowski was evidently much intrigued both by the fresh-sounding primitive unhibitedness of the music (those very qualities, in fact, which scandalised 'civilised' musicians of the time) and by the natural resource and musicianship of the performers. Like Bartók he felt at ease with country people and they reciprocated his affection. He deplored the gradual erosion of their culture, the ousting of their costume by dull, stereotyped urban trends, the playing of waltzes and polkas at weddings instead of traditional highland dances.

Many folk weddings – including that of Mieczyslaw (Jerzy) Rytard and Helena Roj, a mountaineer girl – must have coalesced in the composer's mind when the music for his ballet-pantomime finally began to take shape. The original idea came from Iwaszkiewicz and the Rytards at Zakopane during the winter of 1922–3, and was furthered by a commission from Emil Mlynarski and the Warsaw Opera. Nevertheless, not until 1931 was the full score complete. The first performance took place in Prague in 1934 and proved both a popular and critical success. A number of changes were made for the crisis-fraught Paris première with Lifar in 1936. When the score was

[1] In this respect an important predecessor of *Harnasie* is Grieg's Op. 72 *Slåtter* for piano solo, transcriptions or 'realisations' (in the sense of Szymanowski's own Paganini transcriptions) of traditional Hardanger fiddle dance-music as notated and adapted for solo violin by Halvorsen. Grieg's skill in the *Slåtter* in transferring the wild uncouth beauty of the peasant originals to a new and in many ways alien medium is equalled by Szymanowski's in *Harnasie*; another link is the predominance of the sharpened fourth of the scale in both Polish and Norwegian (and in Hungarian) folk music. John Horton in his Master Musicians *Grieg* (p. 125) comments that, although Grieg supplies a basis of functional harmony, this is combined 'in a remarkably daring way with the non-functional dissonances of the traditional style, producing an entirely new harmonic perspective, unique of its kind until the appearance of Bartók's folk-music arrangements and improvisations'. This is very much part of the historical background to *Harnasie*.

published Szymanowski provided special endings for some of the individual dances and cued the vocal solos and pistol-shots into instruments, so that a concert performance minus extras is feasible.

Harnasie is Szymanowski's only work to employ authentic Tatra folksongs on an extended scale, some from his own (lost) collection. Oddly, perhaps, he never set any for voice and piano or chorus, as he did in the case of the *Twelve Kurpian Songs* for the former combination, and the *Six Kurpian Songs* for the latter.[1]

Szymanowski explained his adoptive, protective attitude to Góral music in an interview given at the time of the Prague première of *Harnasie* in 1935: 'You ask me why I chose a rural theme . . . it is a question of strong attachment to the people of the Podhale region, a kind of adopted birthplace of mine . . . certain peasant cultures being destined to become extinct, we artists have the duty of preserving them for posterity. . . .' He did not believe in the 'mechanical translation' of folksongs into an alien medium; rather should they be 'sublimated', their essence extracted and re-created in a new art-form.

Clearly Szymanowski was strongly attracted to the 'exotic' element of this music, just as he had earlier been drawn to the exoticism of the Orient. In an article on Góral music published in *Muzyka* in 1930 he drew attention to the distinction between Polish lowland and highland music, surmising that the prevailing impression of the highlanders as unmusical 'sprung from the lowland "intelligentsia", because they were horrified by the yells and resounding cries of the young shepherds calling to each other across high mountain ledges. These calls cannot be said to have anything in common with the gentle *bel canto* of gondoliers overheard on Venetian canals.' Szymanowski relates the special character of Góral music both to 'the unrelenting severity of life in the mountains' and to 'the intoxicating beauty of the surrounding landscape', the Górals being far more conscious of their environment than the lowland

[1] These songs belong to a small region of Poland north-east of Warsaw on the border of East Prussia. Szymanowski may have seen performances by a Kurpian folk-group in Warsaw in 1928, but he had no direct knowledge of the area or its music; he drew for the latter on Wladyslaw Skierkowski's collection, *The Kurpian Forest in Sound*. The theme of the *Variations on a Polish Theme*, Op. 10, was a Tatra melody taken from the collection of Jan Kleczynski, a nineteenth-century critic who made a special study of Polish highland music.

peasantry. Working with Góral music was, for Szymanowski, like 'hewing out ideas' from 'impregnable and primitive granite'.

Now delicacy, an exquisite fineness, is the attraction of Szymanowski's impressionist works; that he is here drawn to a more rugged music, a more massive, less finished art – folk-art – is not only through sympathy with the more obvious qualities of ruggedness and masculinity, but also because he divines the sweetness, the vulnerability, which lies at the heart of the strength. Once we realise this, our eyes are opened to new dimensions of affinity between, say, the Third Symphony and *Harnasie*, just as the 'primitivism' of the Stravinsky of *Le Sacre du Printemps* and the 'civilisation' of Debussy's Impressionism are by no means mutually exclusive. In every case we find short, hypnotic melodic phrases, often of folksong origin, in incantatory repetition; non-developing formal processes; static harmonic textures; ostinati and repetitive rhythms which tend to destroy the temporal sense and break on occasion into complex, ecstasy-inducing rhythms of a kind more redolent of oriental than occidental music.

As we know, Szymanowski's interest in folksong as a composition base was in part stimulated by *Le Sacre du Printemps* and what he knew of *Les Noces*, and the themes both of spring awakening and of peasant wedding rites are present in the scenario of *Harnasie*. Yet if we compare the latter, first with *Le Sacre* and then with a ballet like Khatchaturian's *Gayaneh* which is firmly ensconced in the late nineteenth-century Russian nationalist–romantic tradition, it immediately becomes apparent that for all its infinitely greater sophistication, subtlety and integrity as a composition Szymanowski's score has rather more in common with Khatchaturian's than with Stravinsky's. In fact, as far as the latter is concerned it is significant that the influence of *Le Sacre* and *Les Noces* in *Harnasie* is superficial compared with that of *Petrushka*, whose treatment of folk material is still relatively conventional – the folk melodies here (as in *Harnasie*), decked out as they may be in all manner of *nouveau-riche* orchestral finery and splendour, retain their identity as direct quotations. *Petrushka* had evidently been lurking in Szymanowski's unconscious ever since he first heard it in Vienna in 1913. Having put in an interim appearance in *Masques*, it is a notable colouristic force in *Harnasie*, and not only in the burlesque episodes; Szymanowski refers quite clearly to the mysterious *tour de passe-passe* section (much admired by Debussy) at the beginning of the mime-scene where Harnas first sees the bride-to-be and is impressed by her beauty.

The after-effects of Szymanowski's impressionist orchestral style are much in evidence in *Harnasie*, less so in other orchestral scores of his last period; just how ultra-refined is the orchestration, even in the rowdiest tuttis, is brought home to one if, immediately after hearing *Harnasie*, one listens to the Ural wedding-music ('Ural Rhapsody') in Prokofiev's ballet *The Stone Flower* (1948–53). Here is subject-matter similar to that of *Harnasie*, and a twentieth-century composer who employs authentic folk material in much the same way. Yet one is struck immediately by the crudeness (in the non-pejorative sense) of Prokofiev's scoring. A more kindred spirit is Bartók, many of whose folksong-oriented orchestral scores contain impressionistic pages (e.g. *Two Pictures*, *Bluebeard's Castle*, *The Wooden Prince*, *Dance Suite*, *Hungarian Pictures* and the *Cantata Profana*). Frequently the *Harnasie* orchestra shimmers and glitters as if in the afterglow of *King Roger*, and other features of Szymanowski's mature style make some extraordinary virtues out of the necessity of accommodating the new *donnée*, folksong. The bagpipe-drone itself implies a primitive form of bitonality, the principle of which as we know has long been governing Szymanowski's harmonic thinking; what more natural than that, in *Harnasie*, the latter should come to seem a natural extension and amplification of the former? Similarly counterpoint, breath of life and quickening spirit in Szymanowski, is no less vital a force in *Harnasie* than any other major score, as we shall see forthwith.

According to Tatra legend the 'Harnasie' were a band of derring-do highland brigands, named after their leader, Harnas. In the ballet a young girl is being married against her will to a rich elderly farmer. She is rescued in the nick of time by Harnas, with whom she falls in love and whose life she decides to share. Szymanowski tells this simple tale in two tableaux framed by a prologue and epilogue. The prologue, 'On the mountain pasture', is a picture of spring or early-morning awakening, modelled on, though quite different technically from, the introduction to *Le Sacre du Printemps*. The opening pages evoke for Jim Samson 'the bleak, desolate beauty of the Carpathians': a distant solo oboe over a bagpipe-like cello drone sounds the Sabala motif (see Ex. 14 overleaf).

Ex.14 *Harnasie*
Andante tranquillo

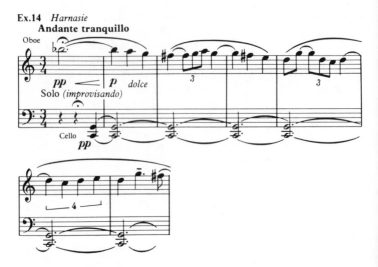

Other instruments respond to it one by one as to a summons, all with their own variant of the 'Sabala', until a teeming, proliferating heterophony fills the air. (Throughout the score the folksong-derived melodies and motifs show a tendency to growth and change strongly reminiscent of that undergone by folksong in the course of oral transmission.) When finally the drone is dislodged, bleating noises in flutter-tonguing brass (*à la Don Quixote*) and a jingle of *Alpenglocken* herald the approach of the sheep as they are driven from their shelters in the valleys to the mountain pastures; a soft woolly *pizzicato ostinato* for lower strings – a counterpoint of different rhythms – marvellously suggests their tumbling and jostling. One element introduced almost casually in a complex, dissonant texture is an oboe melody later to become the song of love and sorrow in the epilogue. In the last bars of the prelude a highland band or *kapel* is heard afar off, another foretaste of later developments. After a pantomime in which the bride-to-be dances with her companions, two pistol shots announce the arrival of the brigands and set the tempo of their march; the solo tenor's song (in which, as in most of the score's other melodic material, the sharpened fourth of the scale is very prominent) comes from Stanislaw Mierczynski's *Music of the Podhale* (1930),[1] a collection of 101 tunes and airs arranged for the

[1] 'Podhale' means the northernmost part of the Tatra mountains.

peasant band of two violins and bass (and to which Szymanowski contributed a preface). The words exult in the violence which is part of the outlaw life.

The vigorous and muscular marching-dance which follows is based primarily on this tune, often juxtaposed or combined with another, of which much more is heard in the second mime-scene, where Harnas meets the bride and is struck by her beauty. The obnoxiously boorish groom arrives (hideously gaping trombone glissandi). Musically this scene is typical of the quasi-symphonic quality of integration Szymanowski achieves throughout the score: he not only resumes, develops and recapitulates material from the previous section but harnesses it in rhythmic as well as melodic counterpoint with a new theme. A cymbal crash introduces the 'Brigands' Dance', a stylisation of the 'Zbojmicki' – a group dance for men holding *ciupaga* (the long-handled hatchets of the high-landers) which they whirl and catch with a flourish. This can be clearly heard in Szymanowski's music, as can the many leaping and crouching movements of which the dance is composed. Popular Góral melodies again form the basis of the music; one of them, later elaborated in a fugal build-up, had already been used by Paderewski in his *Tatra Album* for piano (1884). In the second tableau pre-nuptial celebrations are in full swing, the orchestra trills and glissandoes its glee, but the words of the massive, declamatory two-part chorus (a melody collected by Szymanowski himself) are ironic, for they express the repugnant feelings of the bride at the prospect ahead of her: 'I would not object if the fast-flowing water were to carry you away tomorrow, for you are not mine and I am not yours. . . . Janek is my love, and it is of him I would rather sing.'

Two other Góral tunes alternate with Ex. 15 and combine with it in inebriatedly vociferous counterpoint; more explicit of the true situation is the melancholy pathos of the bride's theme as she enters, a

Ex.15 *Harnasie*

Góral version of a famous Polish wedding song. A reprise of 'Janek is my love' leads into the drinking-song which Szymanowski originally set in 1924 for voice and piano. The splendid 'Mountaineers' Dance' which follows is an elaborate stylisation in symphonic terms of the *kapel*, and the last great manifestations in Szymanowski's output of the Dionysian impulse, of what Percy Grainger termed the 'athletic and ecstatic intoxications that inspire, and are inspired by, the dance'. The swish and swirl of dance-movements, the entry of more and more participants in the dance, an ever-increasing animation and exuberance – all seek a natural outlet in heterophony and polyphony, in the continual crowding-in of new melodic ideas (many of them authentic tunes from the Mierczynski collection), in the unbroken rhythmic 'keeping-on-ness' (Grainger), in bitonal harmony which sounds completely in character, a logical outcome of the highland idiom with its many inbuilt dissonances.

With the re-entry of the wedding-song the music careers to its climax, but abruptly disintegrates upon the arrival of Harnas and his men. The last dance, in which the guests are routed and the bride carried off, begins with an *appassionato* statement of the brigands' theme, and employs both orchestrally and chorally two more sturdy masculine Góral tunes set below a 'continuously spinning line' (Wightman) on high violins, as in the last movement of the *Symphonie Concertante*; the first generates an enormous accumulation of power at the main climax:

Ex.16 *Harnasie*

The music of the final tableau, set in the forest by the side of a lake, is Szymanowski's most limpidly beautiful, a setting for tenor solo and orchestra of a Tatra love-song (again from Szymanowski's own collection) which anticipates sorrow as well as joy:

> Every night in ecstasy, every day in anguish,
> If you love me as I love you;
> We shall become as angels in the heavens
> If you love me as I love you.

Pools of a vast, rapt silence gradually envelop the music (the spirit, though not the letter, is that of the end of *Les Noces*), and ripples of a marvellously spaced B major chord bring the work to a radiant, serene close.

From the purely musical point of view *Harnasie* is an exhilarating experience: with its vivid, virile melodies, sculpted toughness of outline and magnificent blaze of primary colours (unusual textures involving the piano are only one aspect of its non-routine orchestral virtuosity), it sounds like mountains look, like mountain air feels and tastes. It is one of the most successful twentieth-century attempts (in Eric Sams's witty phrase) to 'crossfertilise culture with agriculture'; and if we imagine it complemented by vigorous yet poetic choreography, Polish highland scenery and the splendour of authentic Tatra costumes, we must surely hope that the future will bring us the occasional opportunity to see it on the stage. Meanwhile, a touching epilogue in the words of Krystyna Dabrowska who left an evocative account of Szymanowski's funeral in her *Karol of Atma* (Warsaw, 1958):

At the Skalka, in the crypt of the great, they bade him a last farewell. . . . I remember only that after many speeches, when the cathedral was emptying and the people beginning to disperse, they started to play: Andrzej Slodyczka (first violin), Jan Obrochta (second violin), Stanislaw Obrochta (double-bass). And old Mroz on the bagpipes.

1925–6: STABAT MATER

When Stravinsky visited Warsaw in May 1965 Robert Craft recalled that, at a reception given by the Union of Composers, 'again and again I.S. is asked for details about Szymanowski, whose *Stabat Mater*, written in the shadow of the *Symphony of Psalms*, is thought hereabouts to compare not unfavourably with it; but Szymanowski was more V's [Vera's] friend than I.S.'s, and she has not come to the party.'[1]

For once, however, the redoubtable Mr Craft's chronology is at fault, for the *Symphony of Psalms* was composed in 1930, some four or five years *after* the *Stabat Mater*. It is worth laying this particular ghost, but in any case the stiffly hieratic grandeur of Stravinsky's work has no more in common with the expressive, introspective intimacy of the *Stabat Mater* than has the latter with the Byzantine ceremonial of *King Roger*. Both *Stabat Mater* and Janáček's *Glagolitic Mass* set liturgical texts in the vernacular; but, again, the latter is a public utterance made *con bravura* and with many an extrovert festal flourish, whereas the former is a personal expression of grief which, though sublimated in quasi-religious terminology, remains in essence a private document. This is explained by the circumstances of its composition. In 1924, when Szymanowski was in Paris, the Princesse de Polignac asked him for a choral–orchestral work with soloists, perhaps using a Polish text – a kind of Polish requiem. Originally Szymanowski had in mind a 'peasant requiem' – 'something peasant and ecclesiastical (in the style of "St Francis" of the *Słopiewnie*), naively devotional, a sort of prayer for souls . . . a mixture of simple-minded religion, paganism and a certain austere peasant realism'. The text was to be the work of Iwaszkiewicz.

Obviously to accommodate such a scheme, a drastic simplification of Szymanowski's musical language would be called for. This he achieved partly through study of sixteenth-century sacred music (particularly Polish), partly through an ever-increasing familiarity with Polish folksong. Both tended to re-establish in Szymanowski the expressive staying-power of pure, clear-water diatonic and triadic formulae. That the two are closely related is later borne out by the fact that the harmonic language of the *Stabat Mater* is later re-employed in certain of the settings of Kurpian folksongs – both in the *Six Kurpian Songs* for unaccompanied chorus (1928) and the *Twelve Kurpian Songs* for voice and piano (1930–2). The affinity is particularly close in those songs which bear some heavy emotional burden and whose meaning and feeling Szymanowski enhances to poignant effect – the two bridal songs of parting in the choral group

---

[1] *Stravinsky: Chronicle of a Friendship 1948/1971*, p. 275. Though Szymanowski and Stravinsky were good friends in later years, Szymanowski was even closer to Vera Sudeikina (later Stravinsky's second wife), who used to visit him in his sanatorium at Davos.

(nos. 3 and 5), and, in the voice-and-piano collection, no. 3, in which a young girl expresses anxiety as to her fate in marriage, movingly set to a diatonic, scalic accompaniment of ever-increasing expressive intensity.

Ex.17   Twelve Kurpian Songs, no.3

All these songs involve or imply the sundering of the bond between parents and children, like the *Stabat Mater*. No. 7 expresses the grief of a young girl whose beau has been conscripted and sent abroad, while in no. 9, which admits much the same measure of simple but starkly expressive bitonality as the 'Virgo virginum praeclara' in the *Stabat Mater*, a lover feels remorse over his infidelity.

The *Stabat Mater* is, perhaps, the most searching expression in all Szymanowski of that profound human need to seek roots in a remote past.[1] The musical idiom is austere, severe to the point of bareness; the glittering shop-windows of the West (romanticism and Impressionism) and indeed of the East (exoticism) are all blacked out and the orchestration is monochrome. The orchestra itself is modest in dimensions, like that of all Szymanowski's later works except *Harnasie* and the *Veni Creator* – no trombones or tuba, only two trumpets, double woodwind. The one luxury Szymanowski permits himself is the organ, in the two movements where the tutti is employed; but in this particular context it sounds like a logical extension and amplification of the orchestral sound-palette, its liturgical overtones being of course highly appropriate. 'Archaic' or primitive features abound: the plainsong-like chanting on a mono-tone, modal, melodic contours, ostinati and parallel fifths, thirds and triads which constitute a choral idiom of a primarily homophonic nature, counterpoint being reduced to a minimum.

Szymanowski set a Polish paraphrase of the Latin text by Jozef Janowski which brings all its latent sado-masochism to the fore. This evidently aroused interest on Szymanowski's part – he found in it an expression of immediacy, 'a fine "painting" with the colours recognised and appreciated, as opposed to the mere "outlines" of the classical original' – in what he might otherwise have felt to be a poem *de mortuis in lingua mortua*. Yet to bring any kind of programmatic or illustrative element into his music was the reverse of his intentions. He sought to *objectify* – both the familiar constituents of his musical style and the tragedy of the Passion itself. Emotion is veiled in reticence, not flaunted in outpouring. Drama and tension are built into the music itself; nothing crudely representational is allowed to obtrude. In the 'Quis est homo qui non fleret' what are we to make of the deep dull, offbeat thuds in the bass and the tolling ninths – distant echoes, perhaps, of the *via dolorosa* or even of the scourging of Christ? The C pedal-point which grinds monumentally, all-subduingly, against the modal B major of the chorus in the 'Virgo virginum praeclara', the other 'dramatic' (in the sense here of vehemently or

[1] Perhaps the most radical manifestation of which is Orff's *Carmina Burana* (1936), written some ten years after the *Stabat Mater*. The drastic simplification of musical means in the latter must have formed part of the seed-bed which nurtured the growth and sudden shooting into blossom of the former, with its eupeptic, iconoclastic return to first musical principles.

violently expressive) movement – both are commanded by the voice of the baritone solo – may perhaps be heard as the booming or humming of bell overtones, but abstruse harmonic colours are employed with as great a restraint as those of the orchestra. Always we are reminded that the *Stabat Mater* is an expression of passion crucified, not triumphant. Melodically, too, the *Stabat Mater* has its own integrity. In this respect it approaches the Rachmaninov of the *Night Vigil* (for *a cappella* choir), particularly of course in the fourth movement ('Fac me tecum pie flere') in which the orchestra is silent and the harmony exclusively triadic. The two solo voices – soprano and contralto – rise now and then out of the ensemble with exquisite effect, often filling in 'holes' left for the purpose in the harmonic texture of the chorus:

Ex.18 *Stabat Mater*

That Szymanowski also possessed the gift of Britten, Berstein and Orff in refracting ordinary triadic harmony at a hitherto unsuspected angle is aptly demonstrated in the last movement, 'Christe, cum sit hinc exire' (see over).

In Szymanowski's desire to achieve a 'religious' music whose character bore no taint of 'official' or 'artistic' piety of the kind he disliked and which had not been artificially inseminated by folksong (he alludes to rather than quotes from the latter, to the liturgical Gregorian 'Stabat Mater' and to the *Gorzkie żale*, the traditional Polish lenten songs of lament which meant much to him), we are reminded of Rachmaninov's 'conscious counterfeit of the ritual' and of the uniquely personal religious quality he distils in the *Night Vigil*,

Ex.19 *Stabat Mater*

despite – or rather because of – the fact that neither were worshippers in the conventional sense of the term. A similar 'uniquely personal religious quality' is to be found only once in Szymanowski's work outside the *Stabat Mater*, and that is in the *Litany to the Virgin Mary* (1930–3) which sets two of the seven stanzas of a poem by Jerzy Liebert ('Twelve-toned Cithara' and 'Like a Dwarf Bush'). The composer had a high regard for these two fragments whose musical language is very similar to that of the *Stabat Mater*; and both works gain immeasurably from being performed (or recorded) in the liturgical context to which they belong not only spiritually but also – and the two are inseparable – in terms of the music's 'physiological' or technical constitution.

That the projected 'Peasant Requiem' was ultimately superseded by the *Stabat Mater* (completed 1926) was due both to a request on the part of a Warsaw businessman, Bronisław Krystall, for a work in memory of his wife Izabela, and to the accidental death in January 1925 of the composer's niece Alusi Bartoszewiczowna, the daughter of his sister Stanislawa. Stasia was in fact one of the soloists in the first performance, which was given by Fitelberg in Warsaw in January 1929. That in this country it found its way so quickly into a Three Choirs Festival programme (Worcester, 1932, with Elgar and G. B. Shaw in the audience) testifies to its approachability (which is not synonymous with conventionality) of idiom.

1927: SECOND STRING QUARTET

For all his veneration for Mahler, Szymanowski was a personally reticent composer; his music is not exhibitionistic or autobiographical, and ecstasy rather than agony is its keynote. Yet from 1916 on the composer had much to agonise over. The ageing process in itself tends to be feared and resented more by homosexual people than others, particularly those who, like Szymanowski, seem unable or unwilling to form stable relationships; and when this emotional insecurity is exacerbated by constant money worries and, in the end, an irreversible breakdown in health, the picture is a grim one indeed. It is hard not to hear the Second String Quartet as at least in part a cry of distress, an expression of bitterness and frustration. This is particularly true of the second and third movements, the first being more in the nature of nostalgic reminiscence: melodic, harmonic and textural features of the impressionistic period advance only to vanish in mists and dimness. But the second and third movements confront us very forcibly with the present in the guise of Tatra folk music. There is, however, one crucial conceptual difference between this music and the *Twenty Mazurkas*, Op. 50 (1924–5), which cross-breed the traditional dance-forms of the mazurka as defined and stylised by Chopin – the *mazur*, the *oberek* and the *kujawiak* – with the melodic idiosyncrasies (and related harmonies) of Góral music, thus bringing both into a wider perspective. In so doing Szymanowski was consciously raising a monument to Polish nationalism, attempting to create the basis for a national style that should transcend the specifically regional – much like Bartók, in fact, whose apparent influence on *Harnasie*, the *Mazurkas* and this quartet may be at least in part more a matter of coincidental affinity of style and idea. But in the Second Quartet one feels that Góral music has for once become the means to a purely musical end, has ceased to function as a consciously nationalist entity. The sardonic savagery of the second movement suggests as much, with the brutal open fifths (often involving open strings), misshapen ostinati, pizzicati flying like splinters or pieces of grit, and fractured, frenetic *oberek*-style rhythms all contributing to the notion of a kind of post-Mahlerian dance-of-death.

Compare too the opening of the first of the *Mazurkas* with that of the quartet's finale. Both employ variants of the 'Sabala' motif familiar to us from the *Słopiewnie* and *Harnasie* (see Ex. 14, p. 84); but whereas in the mazurka it asserts itself very positively *as* the 'Sabala' – over an open-fifth drone which is just as positively a stylisation of the bagpipes – in the quartet it has become *in toto* Szymanowski's personal property, the subject, in fact, of an intense and concentrated fugue. There can be no mistaking the spirit of anguish – of agony, in fact – which finds expression here. After the first furious onslaught the music disintegrates in limping fragments, but life quickly stirs amid the ruins. The conflict when it resumes is even fiercer than before, but the outcome is victory, with the 'Polish' D sharps in a bright, unequivocal A major magnificently asserting the sweetness of life even in the face of physical adversity.

1932–3: SYMPHONIE CONCERTANTE AND SECOND VIOLIN CONCERTO

Though impressionist and folklorist elements are to be found in both these works, their basic orientation is neo-classical. Their remoteness from the stylistic world of Szymanowski's impressionist period is exemplified by the fact that precisely the ideal recording acoustic for, say, the 'romantic' Third Symphony – which needs a rich, warm, spacious, deep-focus sound – would spell (indeed *has* spelled) disaster for the 'classical' *Symphonie Concertante*, which can thrive only in clean, dry conditions with a minimum of reverberation.

Szymanowski made his Op. 60 an orchestral piece with piano obbligato rather than a virtuoso concerto because he wrote it for himself to play. Though a very able pianist he was no Rachmaninov or Prokofiev, and in any case, as we have seen, he was never interested in technical brilliance *per se*, in whatever medium. He frequently gave the piano as an orchestral instrument roles of an above-average importance (e.g. in both Violin Concertos, the Third

Symphony and *Harnasie*), so the *Symphonie Concertante* can be seen as a logical large-scale outcome of this tendency.

Szymanowski wanted the *Symphonie Concertante* to be not only readily performable by himself but accessible to his audience. So the piece is designedly one to be enjoyed by both performer and listener, whereas the graver tone of the Second Violin Concerto represents, one imagines, a repository of the composer's deep personal feelings for Kochański. However, Szymanowski was too conscientious an artist ever self-consciously to 'write down' to anyone, and the 'popular' features of the *Symphonie Concertante* – the main theme of the first movement with its interpolated yodel, the subtly sensuous, quasi-nocturnal orchestration of the slow movement, the exuberant dance-like charge of the finale – all are inherent in Szymanowski's mature style anyhow. Formally, too, the work is straightforward: it is the only one of Szymanowski's concertos to adopt the classical three-movement plan, but the composer cannot resist the occasional deflection from the prescribed path, e.g. by making the first movement virtually monothematic – the 'development' does not 'develop' the main theme but instead creates a new theme immediately from it – and by making the climax of the slow movement the return of its main theme in an anguished transformation almost painful in its intensity: one which contrasts as violently as can be with, and is barely recognisable from, the gentle flute and viola colloquy at the outset. This is a sustained melodic flight equalled in Szymanowski only by the first movement of the Second Violin Concerto (Ex. 20).

Ex.20 *Symphonie Concertante*

At the end the piano, which has hitherto kept a low but decorative profile, comes to the fore in a birdsong-like cadenza and links up with the rondo-finale. This clearly reflects Szymanowski's admiration for Prokofiev's Third Piano Concerto, both in its ebullient rhythmic drive and the percussive brilliance of its writing for the solo instrument (not to mention the quasi-Gogolian cock-snookery of the E flat clarinet which has already had some brief but acid comment to make in the *scherzando* section of the first movement's recapitulation). The prevailing dance-rhythm is that of the *oberek*, and the rondo-theme also incorporates the familiar folksong-inflected sharp fourth, F sharp in the key of C major:

Ex.21 *Symphonie Concertante*

As the movement gathers momentum it attracts elements of an occasionally rougher, almost gypsy-like character; but a telling point-of-repose is provided by a cool, mazurka-like episode. The final pages generate a quasi-Dionysian frenzy which propels the music from one pinnacle of rhythmic excitement to the next, and which finds expression also in an obbligato of wildly shooting, flailing lines for high unison violins with stinging open-stringed acciaccature thrust in wherever possible – perhaps an idealisation or apotheosis of the Tatra mountaineer fiddling which Szymanowski so much admired.

The *Symphonie Concertante* was first performed in Poznán in October 1932 with the composer at the piano and Fitelberg conducting. It quickly became popular (the fact that the finale was not infrequently encored raised doubts in the hyper-self-critical Szymanowski as to its quality!), other enthusiastic early exponents being Jan Smeterlin and Rubinstein, its dedicatee. Parts of a Szymanowski–Fitelberg performance in Copenhagen in January 1933 were recorded and enable us to form some idea of the former's pianistic qualities. What is clear to hear, both on this recording and that of two mazurkas from Opp. 50 and 62, is his velvety softness of touch, the warmth and flexibility of his phrasing and his refusal in a lyrical context to submit to any tempo-ral straitjacket. As we would expect he was an intensely *musical* performer. He must have been a difficult soloist to follow, but his view of the cadenza in the first movement of the *Symphonie Concertante* is certainly worth study, particularly for those who aspire to play it themselves.

In the Second Violin Concerto the relationship between soloist and orchestra is no less close than in the *Symphonie Concertante* or the First Concerto. The textures are so contrapuntally close-knit that the soloist in effect is part of the orchestra, and to balance them apart, with the former stealing all the limelight and the latter reduced to the level (both literally and metaphorically) of a vaguely defined accompanimental background, is to offer the listener a lecture or harangue rather than a discussion. Like the First Concerto, the Second is in one continuous movement; here, however, the periods are more sharply defined, even if Szymanowski is still relatively non-conformist in his architectural policies. The opening of the First Concerto has been duly admired, but the way in which its successor unfolds is in its way no less masterly: its first twenty-six pages constitute, in effect, one enormous lyrical paragraph, never a break in the song:

Ex.22   Violin Concerto No.2

After the cadenza the *molto energico* finale (a sonata-rondo) launches the soloist on a theme which immediately returns us to the astringent sound-world of the Tatra mountaineers:

Ex.23   Violin Concerto No.2

Here – in heavily stylised form, of course – is an apotheosis of the virtuoso folk-style of Bartek Obrochta's 'violin trio'; and when, as frequently happens, Ex. 23 is let loose among the woodwinds, it breeds so prolifically as to form an agreeable multi-voiced, bagpipe-like cacophony. For a while the *kapel*-sounds recede to permit the introduction of a fully-fledged second subject whose passionate singing line is exquisitely offset by piano filigree and trilling strings (even in his post-impressionist scores Szymanowski likes to dissolve the outline of his strings, when they function purely as harmonic support, into feathery insubstantiality *via* trills or the finger tremolo). The concerto's climax arrives with the triumphant homecoming of the main theme (Ex. 22), held, as it were, shoulder-high by the highlanders' music which, in the coda, flings to a wild and abandoned – yes, Dionysian – conclusion.

Kochański played the new Concerto only once – with the Warsaw Philharmonic, conducted by Fitelberg. He was already suffering an advanced abdominal cancer when he was working on the piece with Szymanowski, and he died soon after its first performance. Zofia Kochańska held the composer, who adored her, partially responsible and never forgave him.

Conclusion

The idea of the cosmopolitan gentleman aesthete, the moneyed aristocratic thinker, the sophisticated traveller and cultivated *bon viveur* with the means to indulge all his whims, whether gastronomic, cultural or sexual – this tends to provoke derision today. But Szymanowski is the exception that proves the rule. Iwaszkiewicz has confirmed that throughout his life Szymanowski aspired to the condition of the renaissance man, the *homo universalis*. He peddled no narrow specialism but believed that musicians should be broad-reading and broad-thinking, an outlook which also determined his policies as a teacher. He steeped himself in music, literature, history and philosophy (particularly that of Germany and Islam), folk-cultures and the fine arts, and placed his accumulated knowledge at the service of his literary and musical creations: hence the fabulous historico-mythological resonance of *King Roger*, the mystic distillation of *The Song of the Night*, the blend of empathy and ethnic authenticity which makes *Harnasie* such a fine audiovisual experience.

With so much going in his favour, why the disappointment that is the prevailing tone of Szymanowski's history? Why was a man of such talent and personability (his charm is averred by Vladimir Dukelsky (alias Vernon Duke), himself a practised dispenser of that commodity; in his autobiography *Passport to Paris* he refers to Szymanowski's 'irresistibly Polish polish, catlike suavity and softness of speech') so often thwarted in his lifetime? Why was he not accepted as the leader of Polish music, even in the absence of other contenders for the role? The fault lies not in our stars but in ourselves, saith the Bard, and Szymanowski had inherited from his father not only artistic ability but a strain of practical incompetence and financial irresponsibility which was to spell disaster in the last years of his life. Even before the Revolution family money, though available, was never in plentiful supply; after it Szymanowski at the age of nearly forty had to face the necessity of supporting himself virtually unaided. That he enjoyed the good things of life is vouched for by the essentially hedonistic quality of his music; but expensive tastes, once acquired, are not so easily renounced, and Szymanowski continued to indulge them long after the wherewithal to do so no longer existed.

Unfortunately a man who cannot organise the practical side of his own life can scarcely be expected to direct or control that of others; and Szymanowski's was not that kind of personality. He was too private ever to be public; he never had the knack, as Britten for instance had, of somehow galvanising the world around him into purposeful activity on his behalf. He was not a natural leader: we have, significantly, no record of his ever conducting – did he perhaps try and fail? Insecurity and shyness seem often to have caused problems. Perhaps it is true that his proneness to pepper his scores with detailed expression marks and instructions to performers is a manifestation of a basic insecurity; this would link him not only with Mahler but also with Britten. Or is it in each case merely the professional's perfectionist urge to forestall misinterpretation and the ravages of insensitivity or poor musicianship on the part of performers? Perhaps too it is more than coincidence that the principal media for which Szymanowski composed were all re-presented by musicians he knew and trusted from his childhood days: the piano (Rubinstein), the voice (his sister Stasia), the violin (Kochański) and the orchestra (Fitelberg). All served him well during his lifetime, and those who outlived him remained loyal to his music.

It was, however, typical of Szymanowski's professionalism that once he had undertaken an uncongenial task – e.g. the directorship, first of the Warsaw Conservatory, then of the State Academy of Music – he exerted himself to the utmost on behalf of those to whom he felt a responsibility. (Similarly he was often concerned to provide financial support for younger musicians or members of his family even at times when his own situation had reached crisis point.) One imagines that he was liked by his students as much as we know he was detested by those of his colleagues who, in common with many teachers, were more interested in personal prestige than in the well-being of those in their charge. From the purely musical point of view, however, he was too much of a traditionalist to appeal in any great degree to the emerging Polish avant-garde who turned more in the direction of Stravinsky and *Les Six*.

Szymanowski is excellent value. He is both a composer who communicates clearly and composes supremely well. Quality awaits one at every turn; musicians whom professional commitments have caused to familiarise themselves with works they might otherwise have ignored for ever have been surprised and delighted at what they have discovered. He had no time for gratuitous note-spinning or academic cerebration – even his complex fugal structures have an expressive and humanistic, as opposed to a purely intellectual, purport. His music is firmly based in classical and romantic practice and in forms, textures and characters of instruments as they are traditionally understood; and as classicist, romanticist, impressionist, folklorist, even neo-classicist, he has something for everyone interested in early twentieth-century music. He was an eclectic but was saved from the defects and dangers of an assiduous cultivation of *manner* by the fact that he had at all times a *matter* to present, a personal vision, a poetic apprehension of what, to him, were the realities of life, and a fine measure of strength, originality and beauty.

Bibliography

Chylińska, Teresa: *Karol Szymanowski*, trans. A. T. Jordan, New York, 1973 (a 'life in pictures').

Maciejewski, Bogusław: *Karol Szymanowski, his Life and Music*, London, 1967.

Maciejewski, B. and Aprahamian, F. (ed.): *Karol Szymanowski and Jan Smeterlin: Correspondence and Essays*, London, 1970.

Samson, Jim: *The Music of Szymanowski*, London, 1980.

Wightman, Alistair: *The Music of Karol Szymanowski*, unpublished D.Phil. thesis, University of York, 1972.

Index